HEAVEN
Is Closer than You Think
You Think

Love Letters to the World

Volume 2

Fred Blom

ISBN 978-1-63961-900-9 (paperback)
ISBN 978-1-63961-901-6 (digital)

Christian Faith Publishing, Inc.
832 Park Avenue
Meadville, PA 16335
www.christianfaithpublishing.com

Printed in the United States of America

Contents

Foreword

———— ❧ ————

This is a testimony of real life, not games or movies. The majority of the people in the world don't believe in the one and only God. Then there are fewer who believe in Jesus Christ. Of that group, how many drift in and out of this commitment? How many worship with their lips, but not their hearts? My parents and relatives fell into the group of "there is no God, just nature and the natural renewal of its cycle." For me, curiosity was the thing. I had to know the beginning and end of everything, step by step. It's the way I am built! I want every breath and every step I take to be closer to Jesus Christ. Walk with me, and we will see how close heaven really is to us. Run away with me, and I bet we will run right into the hand of God. I have done it a couple of times! I want you to come with me! Please, it's important!

Why write this testimony of life? Did I say please, come along with me? Well, we all have the happy and sad, the hard and easy, and the close to God, whether we are aware of it or not, and the far from God, which we do not understand. Just a few weeks ago, I asked my Father in heaven if I should continue to write the first testimonials each month or perhaps even reveal the deep things which have helped me through life. In the process and time of seven days, I was shown how the hidden secrets of heaven work. To me, it's funny, serious, and truthful—this simple thing connecting so many things together, which have occurred in my life.

I work on my testimonial stories at night. It was the hand of God that leads me to do that, no doubt, and you will learn that a little later. There are always more people to give them to than I can accomplish. Maybe I should put them in a book for everyone, Father. I don't have time or know how. I felt something like a tap on the back of my head when I prayed that. I slapped my hand over my mouth, trying to take it back; at the same time, I looked behind myself to see if something had fallen off the wall. I stopped praying, took a big sigh, and went to sleep. Why did I say "too busy"? I wrestled all night with "the secrets of heaven are my Lord Jesus Christ's, but that which he gives us are ours."

> For there is nothing covered that shall not
> be revealed; neither hid, that shall not be known.
> (Luke 12:2)

I was referred to recently as the little lion which would not roar and the lost generation. Then a voice stood up for me and said, "No, this is the one who walks the dusty road."

I wanted to respond, but I fell to the ground in weakness because of the awesomeness around me. I was shown the loss of mankind and told to go forth with the testimony I was given. I cry and pray with great supplication before the heavenly throne of our savior, Jesus Christ. I don't want anyone to be lost!

Love in Christ, Fred

The Image of God

— ❧ —

Thought: A letter for you with as much love as it can carry. May the Spirit of God direct you in all ways, this I pray! To all with love, let's have a testimonial story about when you pray, follow through with faith no matter how bleak it may seem. Not easy, I know! Did I say not easy?

To all with love,

The rain was threatening, but the relaxing forecast was simply to offer a one- to two-inch scattered showers. It was about 8:00 p.m. when I first heard the light pit-pat of raindrops on the roof. My wife, Linda, offered the question as to if we would be able to help paint the house of one of the pastors at our church. "I offered our services last Sunday to help them, Linda reminded me, with a puzzled look on her face. I really want to help them. I really like Pastor Austin and Calli.

"It is supposed to rain through tomorrow morning. Can we paint if it is not raining too hard?" Linda asked.

"We need a dry surface to paint on, so it may be a little later in the morning before we get started," I responded. "It's all good, and we will be okay."

I had no sooner finished my short response than the rain picked up. The rain then found another gear and increased even more. It finally had my attention, so I rose up and walked to the window to have a glance.

"We will not be painting tomorrow," Linda offered in a more alarming tone.

"They need to get this house done this weekend. They are moving to the new campus and don't have any more time. The forecast is one to two inches," I offered in a repeat. "Get her done, and God can send a blast of air to dry the house off."

I again just finished my statement when a huge whoosh arrived. It went from like a trickle when slowly pouring a bucket to a faster pour to tipping the bucket upside down. We can see the interstate and the mall area from our condo. The rains blacken the sky, and it was already nighttime. There was a complete wall of water falling straight down.

"If this continues, we will have six or eight inches of rain in less than an hour," I offered in a gasp of amazement. "The rain shall not beat on my house or all that the hand of God has given to me," I whispered at the stormy night. Jesus Christ is that rock, and I put all that I am into his hands. I pondered the thought of Noah in his ark and how the rain may have come down in this type of vast dumping.

> That ye may be the children of your Father which is in heaven: for he maketh his sun to rise on the evil and on the good, and sendeth rain on the just and on the unjust. (Matthew 5:45)

> And the rain descended, and the floods came, and the winds blew, and beat upon that house; and it fell not: for it was founded upon a rock. (Matthew 7:25)

> And the rain descended, and the floods came, and the winds blew, and beat upon that house; and it fell: and great was the fall of it. (Matthew 7:27)

The rain was offering all its power. I felt a chill as if it was doing more than just raining. Most people would just say it's raining, but I believe the hand of God is in all things. There are battles raging all around us—some we can see, some we can understand, many we do not see or have the wisdom to understand.

The rain decreased after about ten minutes to just a hard rain, which many of us have seen. We could now see the interstate. The traffic was frozen in place as far as the eye could see. The news was starting to reflect the situation. Roofs on buildings had collapsed from the weight of water. Streets were full of water up to cars' headlights. The stories of cars washed off the roads, the impending flooding basements, roads washing out, manhole covers flying off their positions…

The home we were going to paint the next day was to most just a job to paint a house. To me, it was much more. I have seen battles of various kinds. After seeing many, you have the ability to sense some of them.

"Well, the painting is definitely off for tomorrow," Linda said, exasperated.

"Maybe not," I whispered back.

"I see a lot of rain and mud," she responded.

The phone rang, and it was now ten-thirty. An exhausted voice reported that the basement of their home had six inches of water in it. The electricity had gone off, and the sump pump couldn't work.

"The electricity had just come back on and was now pumping." The voice sighed with some chance of hope. "What should I do?"

"I am very sorry for your dilemma." I offered condolence. "Take all the carpet and pad out of the basement as soon as you can. I can help you if you like. Vacuum the rest, and get as many fans as you can to dry it out quickly."

"My brother and I can get the carpet and pad out. We have a wet/dry vacuum. I only have two fans. Is that enough?"

"No, you will need more," I suggested. I will get you more fans first thing in the morning.

I just got off the phone when Linda said there was a text from people we know, and they had water pouring through a kitchen ceil-

9

ing light. Another text came in from another party, and they had water running down their bathroom wall and mirror. I called both of these families and talked to them. I then called the roofing contractor that had put new roofs on these homes less than a year ago. I was a little puzzled at the events taking place. My contractor friend also had the same feeling, but he assured me he would investigate the events as soon as possible. When water comes down so hard, it can run up the roof or not get off as quickly as need be. In both cases, the water went up the roof and through the roof vents. Crazy!

"We will be working on project houses tomorrow," Linda stated.

"Perhaps for a short time," I replied in surrender.

"What about the project houses?" Linda asked.

"We will look into that tomorrow."

I prayed in the night for strength against what I could see as well as what I couldn't see. I felt a chill again. There was a storm all right, but it was more than rain.

"Father in heaven, I am determined to help paint this home tomorrow. Even if I am the only one painting, I shall not be overcome. I shall lay aside all my work and all of my concerns. I fall before. I stand beside you, and I know that you can speak a single word to move mountains."

*****

It was raining in the morning, but we got an early start. We bought the last fans at a store, which were just enough, and made a delivery. We visited a project house and found a small bit of dampness in one corner of the newly finished basement. A neighbor quickly came over and told us how the rain filled the gutters and poured into a window well and filled the water up high on the glass. His power went out, but he had a battery backup. He even had a window well cover on his window. He told us of how the water had filled up our window well in the same way. He had water in his basement; we only had dampness.

The next project house had no water problems. We had one more in Brandon to check out, but I told Linda we should contact Austin about painting.

"It's raining now," Linda replied with a "can't you feel it?"

Austin responded that he had two dry sides.

We were too far away to make the eight starting time, but we would try to be there by ten. At ten, it's still raining on us, so I called Austin, and his response was he had two dry sides. We loaded the equipment and ladders in the rain and drove over to the home.

"What about the other house in Brandon?" Linda asked.

"Let the hand of God deal with that house," I offered quietly. "We are going painting."

"That house has the bad basement walls we haven't fixed yet," she offered.

"I am going to call my friend in Brandon. Our friend responded that they had over four inches of rain in less than an hour. There was a lot of flooding. If your sump pump was working, it might not be too bad."

"Was the sump pump working?" Linda asked.

"No," I replied. There are two pumps, one at each end of the house, but no power to them. They had two sump pumps for a reason."

We arrived at Austin and Calli's home. The rain had stopped, and there were two dry sides to start on. There were also two eager boys by the names of Silas and Emerson. There was plenty of work to be done, and a paint job wasn't the only job. A few small inventions, some rollers and brushes handed out, a few new tools to be instructed to a couple of great boys, and the job progressed nicely. A few more lovely people by the names of Brett, Amy, and Vivian made it even sweeter. There was mud on our feet but paint on our tools. We scrapped while we painted—odd, I know. We dismantled fences and whatnot while we painted—again odd, I know. I wanted this job to be done today! The image of God had shined upon us as the sun began to break through the clouds. I felt appreciation as I whispered praise to my savior, Jesus Christ. To me, God's image is in the face and actions of those who call him Lord.

I heard a call for lunch, as I moved my ladder to a new position.

"Come have some lunch," Austin offered.

We are full of mud. We are a mess," I replied.

"Don't concern yourselves with that," Austin coaxed. "You can wash your hands at the sink."

I returned to the table with many purchased items of food. Everyone was busily helping themselves to the bounty. I bowed my head and folded my hands. I began to pray. This was more than a meal to me. I do not remember the last time I was in someone's home and being offered a meal. I saw the image of God in the love, in prayer, and in the giving of one to another. The spirit of God stirs great emotion in me. I needed to glorify God or go private and shed a tear. I picked up two slices of bread, put some salami on it, and bit it.

Everyone was busy as I whispered, "Father, release me from this situation."

In that instant, Brett drove up with the trailer.

"I will go move my pickup so Brett can back into the driveway," I suggested as I walked out the door. A few tears rolled down my cheek as I whispered, "Father, how close you are."

> And it came to pass, as he sat at meat with
> them, he took bread, and blessed *it*, and brake,
> and gave to them. (Luke 24:30)

The eating of the sandwich was slow as I went back to work. I wanted to remember this sandwich as if it was the last piece of food I may have. The afternoon went quickly as everyone painted or cleaned in the yard. By six, we had a beautiful little home—the gray little house trimmed in white, its carved wooden door, painted a dusty rose, just said COME ON IN. The storms rose, the rains fell, the damages fell where it may, but the image of God prevails in the love of Jesus—the love to one another!

> And Jesus said unto them, "I am the bread
> of life: he that cometh to me shall never hunger;

and he that believeth on me shall never thirst."
(John 6:35)

I have had many people of age tell me through the years that
you should give of your life to others before your needs. My parents
were included in this group even though they didn't profess Jesus as
their savior. The feeling was that you didn't deserve the gift of life if
you couldn't raise others up first. Why not do this within the hand
of our Father in heaven?

> Greater love hath no man than this that a
> man lay down his life for his friends. (John 15:13)

> For all have sinned, and come short of the
> glory of God. (Romans 3:23)

When I reached the project house in Brandon Saturday, I went
into the basement. I expected a dry basement, which was probably
bold of me. The cracked walls, the bowed walls, the nonworking
sump pumps all did their job—or did they? That basement was the
driest of all the folks I had visited with. Trust and obey, for there is
no other way. When my Father in heaven woke me Saturday night to
talk to me, I felt so loved for all he had done for me. I had to get up
and dry my face several times in a two-hour period. To know Jesus
Christ is to serve him!

> For God so loved the world, that he gave his
> only begotten Son, that whosoever believeth in
> him should not perish, but have everlasting life.
> For God sent not his Son into the world to con-
> demn the world; but that the world through him
> might be saved. (John 3:16–17)

Love in Christ, Fred

Where Is My Child?

— ✑ —

June 2013

Thought: A letter for you with as much love as it can carry. May the Spirit of God direct you in all ways, this I pray! Let's have a testimonial story about when you pray, follow through with what is asked of you by the Holy Spirit. Our Father in heaven teaches step by step. Most events are so awesome you can't wrap your head around them. Come on, let's go a little further!

To all with love,

Why a first testimony? Why love your neighbor or a stranger? Giving a good word is a good deed. Be of good courage and faith. I have been requested to do seven letters of healing. This follows the three prayers of life. There were three strangers in three states rising off a bed of what appeared to be certain death. Glory to God! I can't even wrap my head around the awesomeness of this. My hands are open, but why me, Lord? The seven letters of healing are love letters and prayer unto the Holy Spirit for comfort in a time of great pain. Father, let not thy mercy be held back.

I started doing the monthly first testimonials about two years ago. This I did as I felt requested to do by God. I will just say prayer is a two-way street. I then after one year had a phrase given to me which I had not heard in about fifty years. I drove a thousand miles to walk one mile of road and praise God. When we returned from the trip, there were three requests from people we didn't know well.

Actually, the requests were from friends and/or family members for prayers to help ones who were in a very critical state. Linda and I prayed each time immediately upon requests. The answers were all miraculous! These were the three prayers of life. Then the request for seven letters of healing was given to me. Why? *Why* would be a good question, but I will not ask that question at this time. Instead, I will state, "Yes, Lord" and "Ask of me if you will." Love thy neighbor as thyself, for there is a lot of pain in this world.

When I start working on a project house that is usually prior to 1970, I get excited to find a blessing of hope. I had called the objects a carpenter's blessing. Many times the new homeowner would also place an object. You can tell who placed the object. If the homeowner placed the object, it was usually placed with a prayer request for our Father in heaven to bless the home. Sometimes various family members would place something for each one. It would be something that meant something personally. Carpenter placement or family placement doesn't really happen anymore—sad! No object placement, no prayer, and the result is no blessing from our Lord. I happen to have just seven items of blessings. I will send one with each letter of love and prayer.

Supplication means "to petition or entreat someone for something." A passionate zeal and hunger fuels the prayer of supplication. Strictly speaking, supplication is not *another form of prayer* but the attitude and state of our heart that accompanies prayer.

> Heavenly Father, only thou are holy! It is your name I raise above all others. You have loved us with a love that is so deep, you sent your only precious son to redeem us and give us hope from which we were lost. As you have requested of me is to send seven letters of healing, this is number seven. I knew not as to whom you would send my way. I knew there would be pain and grief. I am but thy servant, and I can only do what I can. Let thy Holy Spirit guide me and help me stand in the gap to do what thou will ask. It is I, Father,

the one who would walk the dusty road. I shed my tears for Dawn and Ryan as I write this letter. They have endured a great trial of the affliction of the loss of baby Madalyn. It is of the sin in this world, the torment of Satan going to and fro. Offer thy mercy and healing hand to be upon Dawn and Ryan. Father, I am he who walks into the snowstorm calling upon thy face of mercy. The times of sparing me from certain death have now become uncountable. You have shown me mercy so many times. Even unto one time I am unable to offer enough thank you. You, Lord, have picked me up and set my feet on solid rock. Please set Dawn and Ryan upon solid rock. Your answer to the three life-saving prayers is forever a praise on my lips to your ears. I know baby Madalyn is with you now, for she has not even reached the age of accountability. Father, there is so much pain from the loss of a child. I have deep emotions about the loss of this child. Please show compassion and healing to Dawn and Ryan. Allow me to exalt your name for every prayer you answer. Bind now the affliction of pain and loss, Father! Let your children be of strength and joy! In the name of my beloved Lord, Jesus Christ, let it be so! Let it be so! Amen!

- First healing letter—a mid-age woman with two kids. Very serious depression! She received a small white hen and a small yellow chick. When she was two, she found these same two items while digging in the dirt by her house. The prayer and letter of love have lifted her to new heights of happiness and hope because someone cares!

- Second healing letter—a small boy was given a 1942 copper penny and a valentine card from a 1942 house. The old valentine card said, "Love, Dougie." The little boy is well today. I love the little guy and pray always for his strength.

- Third healing letter—a mother and father who suffered a great loss of their son. I gave them a 1939 comic book, which was concealed in a secret room. The room had various items, which I just couldn't keep. I found it twenty-five years ago. The bits of mouse-chewed letter I found on the floor revealed a faith that was shattered and had to be rebuilt because of the loss due to war. They sent me a nice response—that a day with the Lord is better than a thousand years without.

- Fourth healing letter—He is a man of God and a good-hearted fellow. He has a great loss of his best friend—his wife—to cancer. Our greatest prayer of happiness is our hope for him. We gave the gift of yellowed bank draft on the President's Bank. It was in the 1850s and found in a home I remodeled in Jackson, Minnesota. Captain John Q put this above the header of a concealed door. It used to be the original door, but it was covered up over time. The certificate was toward the inside wall, but the letter he wrote was behind it. It was hardly legible but offered a hope of no more war and a grateful heart that he survived the civil war. I had this item for twenty-six years. I am waiting for the hand of God to deliver his heart with happiness which is overflowing.

- Fifth healing letter—This lovely couple has been affected by the nasty cancer. It is my greatest hope with a prayer of healing and strength to be theirs. My gift is a brass cross with an inscription of BUT AS FOR ME AND MY HOUSE, I WILL SERVE THE LORD. This is from a 1949 house and speaks for itself.

- Sixth healing letter—The loss of a very young child is far greater than an elderly loss. She only knew love and only love to give. Parents that have to deal with months of pain in the unknown prospects of what the results may be have gone through the many long months of struggling, pain, and decision-making for the life of their child. The gift is a child's toy. Seventeen years ago, I remodeled a house in Canton, South Dakota. The house was built in 1868. We decided to put in a new front door. We found a clay marble and a note in the penmanship of a first- or second-grade child: PLEASE BLESS OUR HOME AND THE PERSON WHO GETS MY MARBLE.

- Seventh healing letter—This person was a bit strange to me to receive a letter of hope, prayer, and healing. Just because I can't see it, it doesn't mean it is not there. James was a speaker at our church. He is filled with the Word of God and has a great many things going on. He needs prayer whether he has affliction or not, so it's all good for me.

Bad things happen to good people. That does not mean that Jesus is not with you. That does not mean he will not protect you. Learn from these times, and they will help you or prepare you for some point intended. I have a small amount of explanation for all the times I have had close calls of death, visions, words, etc. I have been told things years before they come into existence. I share them with my wife. She gives me the "Oh, it's interesting." When it happens, she gives the "Oh, wow!" I say this only because we can't see the big picture or end result. It may not be the thing for us to know until the season is right—a season for all things! Lift up the name of the Lord, and be blessed!

To everything there is a season, and a time to every purpose under the heaven: A time to be born, and a time to die; a time to plant, and a time to pluck up that which is planted; a time to kill, and a time to heal; a time to break down, and a time to build up; a time to weep, and a time to laugh; a time to mourn, and a time to dance; a time to cast away stones, and a time to gather stones together; a time to embrace, and a time to refrain from embracing; a time to get, and a time to lose; a time to keep, and a time to cast away; a time to rend, and a time to sew; a time to keep silence, and a time to speak; a time to love, and a time to hate; a time of war, and a time of peace. What profit hath he that worketh in that wherein he laboureth? (Ecclesiastes 3:1–9)

Be careful for nothing; but in every thing by prayer and supplication with thanksgiving let your requests be made known unto God. (Philippians 4:6)

Is any sick among you? Let him call for the elders of the church; and let them pray over him, anointing him with oil in the name of the Lord. (James 5:14)

Again I say unto you that if two of you shall agree on earth as touching anything that they shall ask, it shall be done for them of my Father which is in heaven. (Matthew 18:19)

Helping someone? Sounds great! It was the weekend we were going to help an aunt and uncle build a new addition to their house. They had built their home in 1942, and now they wanted an indoor bathroom. I guess most of us take that for granted. My job was to take the siding off the front of the house, then I had to remove the sheathing off. This outside wall would become an inside wall, take the pieces off so they could be reused. Okay, I can do that. Everyone had their job to do. If you didn't do your job, it meant more for someone else, right? I was almost done when I spotted something red above the entrance doorway.

"What," I whispered to myself. I finished removing the board above the door.

It was a red chocolate-covered cherry box. It was dusty and musty. I quickly cleaned it off with my shirt. What else could I clean it with? I came down off my ladder and slid the cover off the small box. I stared at the hidden treasure. As I started to look through the contents of postcards, the excitement rose.

Suddenly a voice boomed out. "What do you have there?" Uncle Harold questioned.

"It's a box with postcards," I replied.

The big hand reached for the box. "These are postcards from a three-year wedding trip we took in 1939."

"Three years?" I questioned.

"It was like taking a good bit of time off before getting to work," Uncle continued. "I was thirty when I got married. I had been farming on my own for over ten years when I met the most beautiful person in the world. Your aunt was walking down a road as she was going to work. I stopped and offered a ride. She offered to share her lunch. The food was good, and the rest is history."

"Why is this little box inside the wall?" I asked.

"It's not for me to tell," Uncle responded as he took the little box and went into the house.

It was the middle of summer when I was asked if I would stay with Aunt Dorothy for three days and help her while Uncle Harold was gone.

"I would be happy to," I responded.

I worked on painting the small house the first day. Now Aunt Dorothy is almost completely blind and she wanted to help paint her house. It had four-inch siding so I counted up fifteen pieces and put in a small nail. Her first section was about twelve feet from the corner to a window. She had to count the siding pieces, hang onto her paint bucket, and go a little slow—but a very nice job indeed! This could be a good story right here. Wait for it!

Now Dorothy was a cook for over thirty years at the Good Samaritan in Park Rapids, Minnesota. Cooking blind was no problem for her, so after supper, we would talk. No TV, phone, games. Talking or reading for anyone?

Well, I am ten, so let me make a mistake and talk about something I probably shouldn't.

"Aunt Dorothy, tell me about the postcards I found above the door of the house last spring?" I asked.

There was silence as she put her hands on the table and folded them. Her stare had been straightforward but now dropped down to about where her hands were positioned. The silence cut the air so deep I thought I was going to bleed. My mother had given me a small statement before I left: "Don't do anything wrong. Be nice."

After eternity came to an end, I saw a couple of tears roll down Dorothy's cheek. Now the air was cut so deep I couldn't breathe.

"No, no," I requested. "Let's talk about what we are going to do tomorrow."

"We came back from our long trip to build our house. It was the most wonderful time of our lives. You see, I wasn't very pretty, overweight, and in my midtwenties. I had never been on a date. Meeting Harold almost brought me to believe in God. Miracles, you see. No one in our family ever believed or went to church, so I couldn't quite get there.

"When fourteen years rolled by, I was getting sad about not having a child. I prayed for a child many times, but it seemed as though I didn't know how to pray. In the fourteenth year, I became pregnant. It also happens to be the same year your mother was pregnant with you. We were in Hubbard, Minnesota, and your folks were in Georgia. We had great fun writing letters back and forth. The timing was so perfect because we were due very close together. Joy was everywhere until I went into delivery and my daughter died at birth. You were born a couple of days later. I am very sorry to say that I am the happiest and the saddest every time I see you." The blind, sad lady put her arm around me as I sat next to her and cried. I had never seen her with anything but a smile before.

"I want you to have the box of cards, memories, and the most wonderful time of my life," the blind woman offered. "It was the one time in my life I came so close to believing in God. No one in our family or anyone I knew ever believed. I don't really know why. I was past my midtwenties and had never been on a date. I always felt like a misfit. Then walking down a road and sharing a sandwich with Harold from my lunch brought about the most wonderful beginning of my life. When I lost my child, my life was frozen. Then I got diabetes. Now I am blind. I feel like I am cursed."

"Cursed by who or what?" I asked.

There was silence for eternity again. "Life, I guess," the blind woman whispered.

"Pastor Petersen told me God created life," I explained to the blind woman. "So if we blame God, and God created us, we would have no appreciation of him giving us the innumerable odds of even existing. Pastor also says that he gave his son to die for us so that we could have hope for eternal life."

"You are the only one in our family to go to church," she offered as she stared into my soul. Her stare looked like a big question.

My explanation of how a messenger told me that someone would come to see me in three days; they would give me guidance. Three days later, it all came true. I was hooked and wanted more. Life is bigger than I can understand. I don't feel I have the right to reject or dislike the life I was given.

I lost my best friend last spring. The sadness is still with me and will be with me for the rest of my life. The week before her death, she asked me if I had ever accepted Jesus Christ as my savior. I would like to, if you think it is as important as you suggest. So at lunchtime, there were two ten-year-old kids kneeling in the far corner of the playground, asking Jesus to come into my life.

"Forgive me of my sins, protect me, guide me, and thank you for giving your life that I may have hope in the eternal life."

The blind woman cried! She laughed! She hugged! We prayed, and the love from heaven filled her.

Love in Christ, Fred

No One Cares

———— ⁓ ————

July 2013

Thought: A letter for you with as much love as it can carry. May the Spirit of God direct you in all ways, this I pray! Let's look into a testimonial story to show you how paths of each other can cross for a short time.

To all with love,

The idea of going on a vacation should be very appealing. You budget for it, you plan the details for travel, and you get excited about what you will do when you arrive at your destination. What happens when you don't really think you want to go to this destination? What happens when you finally arrive at this place and ask yourself, "Why am I here?"

Last week I arrived at such a place. The weather was warm and my honey was with me, but I felt a chill. Have you ever gone somewhere and you just didn't fit into the surrounding environment?

The place was Las Vegas, and it delivered on its wintertime temperature of seventy degrees. My wife was excited about seeing the three shows she had previously arranged for. She was excited to see the towering expensive structures and experience the thrill and excitement of the nighttime lighting.

I like to listen to some music, but I don't find it appealing to travel a great distance for it or pay a great sum. We have a very different feeling about where God is in our lives.

She was viewing all the things around us as we walked, and my head was asking God, *Why am I here?*

It's early morning to us, but there didn't seem to be anyone around. It was about 8:30 a.m., as we walked along the so-called famous strip. The comments were about what we were seeing and not much more. We had walked about seven or eight blocks when we came upon an escalator not working. My wife made a suggestion to walk around the corner and get the elevator up to the next level so we could cross the street. She was being very thoughtful to me, as to save on a hip, which bothers me from time to time. There was a sudden gust of wind, which brought about a chill. As quick as the wind came, it left. We commented on how we hoped it wouldn't blow like that all day. There hadn't been a breeze yet nor after. For reasons unknown, I was compelled to climb the three flights of stairs in front of us. My head was still talking to God as we climbed the stairs. Okay, I am strange, but we are all related.

We began our assent on the small mountain. In a short time, we reached the summit. As we turned the corner to use the walk overpass above the traffic, my eye caught a very small blanket covered something in the corner.

"Let's stop and see what's going on," I said.

The response to me was to leave them alone because they probably want to live on the street.

"It looks so small. I think it might be a child," I responded.

My wife responded that it is indeed a terrible thing, "but what can you do?"

My problem is that I, of course, couldn't leave well enough alone. I was compelled to climb up the stairs, and this might be the reason. If I had gone up the elevator, I wouldn't have this opportunity. What opportunity?

I walked the twenty feet or so while my wife waited. I had no idea what I was going to do or not do. The small object moved under the thin gray blanket. I saw a piece of cardboard with crayon markings. "I am nineteen and need help to get off the street." There was a small plastic lid with a few coins in it, maybe thirty cents, but mostly

24

pennies. But I wasn't there to count coins. There were several ciga-
rette butts and small bits of trash in the lid.

"Hello," I said.

The small object appeared from under the blanket, but only her
head. She pulled the blanket up under her chin.

"Can I help?" I asked.

"I don't think so," a small voice replied.

"Perhaps I can buy you a couple of meals," I offered.

There was no response, so I removed some money from my
pocket and handed it to her. I wouldn't lay it in the lid but continued
to hold it out to her until a small dirty hand found its way to the
money I was holding.

"Why are you being nice to me?" the little voice asked.

"It's the right thing to do," I replied.

"Everyone hates me, and I have nowhere to go," the little voice
responded. "May God bless you for your kindness" was her next
response as she pulled the blanket back over her head.

It appeared she didn't want to talk anymore. I heard a couple of
sniffles as if she was starting to cry. I was hit by another stiff gust of
wind and a rush of emotion. From a distance away, I heard my wife
respond with, "Let's go. We can't do anything more."

We continued on, and after several blocks, we saw a young man
running ahead of us and quickly diving headfirst into garbage cans. He
grabbed bits of something and shoved it into his pockets. He found
drink containers and quickly drank whatever was in those containers.

"If we can catch up to him, we will buy him a meal," I suggested.

When we were about fifty feet away, he took off running down
an alley to who knows where. We saw a few others trying to play a
musical instrument, and it was deserving of a donation. Some had
notes of donation for beer and some for drugs. I had to pass on those.

We all know that there are cons taking place in the streets. There
are truly good people that have lost their way for some reason or
another. It is not up to us to decide upon the faults, losses, or reasons.
Always do what you can when you can. You may feel inadequate and
a little lost, as I did. It helps you to understand just a little more as
to what love is.

Listen. Always listen for the Holy Spirit, and God will do the rest.

The Holy Spirit is the Great Comforter sent into the world to guide and protect us. It's your way back when you have lost your way. It's your help when you see no help. It may be easier for some to understand this, as myself. I have had a minimum of a dozen times in my life where I shouldn't be here. There is a purpose for everything, and I mean everything. You may see your family as a unit, but if you look closer, you will be able to see that everyone is related. We are all wacky brothers and sisters. Some need a little more help than others.

> So I returned, and considered all the oppressions that are done under the sun: and behold the tears of *such as were* oppressed, and they had no comforter; and on the side of their oppressors *there was* power; but they had no comforter. (Ecclesiastes 4:1)

> But the Comforter, *which is* the Holy Ghost, whom the Father will send in my name, he shall teach you all things, and bring all things to your remembrance, whatsoever I have said unto you. (John 14:26)

Jesus had to die on the cross for our sins and to leave this world for the Comforter, which is the Holy Spirit, to come into this world. God sent his Son into world to give each of us a chance for eternal life. We can accept and believe or reject it. We can say yes or no. I say if you can create the sun you stand under, don't be concerned. If you can't, it's time to do some thinking.

> Nevertheless I tell you the truth; It is expedient for you that I go away: for if I go not away, the Comforter will not come unto you; but if I depart, I will send him unto you. (John 16:7)

We spent most of our time walking and sightseeing. It was our determination that there was a world of missionary work right there in the streets of Las Vegas. One particular casino had a very large parking and landscape of trees in the back of their hotel. As we walked through the trees, which eventually emptied into the parking lot, we saw a limo parked about seventy yards away. That part was not so unusual, but the young man, about twenty-five years old, came running toward us as fast as he could. Linda became alarmed, but I assured her it surely couldn't be anything to be alarmed about. When he was about ten feet away, he threw himself flat on the ground and began to beg for me to spare his life. When I didn't respond, he raised his head a bit to look at us. He was crying very hard, and he continued to beg for his life. Lindy and I just looked at each other and shook our heads.

"Go and sin no more," I replied.

"Unless you change, it will cost you your life," I continued.

He jumped up and walked away backward, as he began to say thank you and that he will change. After he was halfway back to the limo, he turned around and continued to walk slowly, the rest of the way.

We continued on to the back entrance of the hotel without further incident. It was most unusual, but still he was added to my prayers.

Love in Christ, Fred

Lindy's Shoes

August 2013

Thought: A letter for you with as much love as it can carry. May the Spirit of God direct you in all ways, this I pray! To all with love, let's have a testimonial story about when you pray, follow through with what is asked of you by the Holy Spirit. Support the prayers of others; it will help them grow in the Lord. The smallest support in prayer excels the soul.

To all with love,

So Lindy says, "Let us look in the closet to see if we have any extra shoes." She had just donated some shoes two months ago but was eager to give shoes to a good cause. She resorted to them so as to be able to give three pairs. "Oh, I can get by without these even though I was going to keep them. That's not much. How about you?" she asked me.

"Well, a pair of old slippers, no. Work shoes, no. Casual dress shoes, no. Not used tennis shoes, no. *Aha*, a new pair of tennis shoes. These will do just fine. This is not much!"

"Well, you are giving something you wanted after giving a number of pairs away. You have a good heart."

The shoes were put into the large 4 × 8 crate the next Sunday.

"There is still not much in the crate," Linda whispered. When we got home, the question came up again. "What can we do for more?" Linda asked.

"Pray about it?" So we did!

"Aha," Lindy replied a few minutes later. "I will ask the neighbors and my friends for their shoes."

"Really?" I asked, surprised. I laughed at the statement with a picture in my mind of her taking shoes off her friends' feet.

"I guess," she replied as she laughed about the idea of collecting shoes from her neighbors and friends.

"Go for it!"

We prayed, believed, and had an answer. It really can be that simple and quick. Our Father has a sense of humor, so laugh with him.

> Be careful for nothing; but in everything
> by prayer and supplication with thanksgiving
> let your requests be made known unto God.
> (Philippians 4:6)

Now this was a nice start to the day, to say the least. I wonder if we all might feel a little better if we just helped someone around us without expecting anything in return. Just be a small spark of light for Christ, and the action is worth a thousand words. Let the Holy Spirit use your deeds and words in his way, not your way. Wait for it!

By the end of the week, she had thirty-some pairs of shoes. Sweet! I thought I would pray about this some more that Sunday night. We were a little disappointed that the shoe crate didn't have more shoes in it. Now most people don't believe in the details of God's answers to prayers, but I do—down to each breath I take.

"Call upon a stranger where you have given of your shoes before."

I know that sometimes answers to prayers sound like a riddle, but you will know the answer. Just believe and follow through.

We have only given donations of items like this to two places in Sioux Falls. I called the first, and they couldn't help. I offered to buy some shoes, but they had so few. I wanted to leave them for someone else. I called the second one, which was actually pulling at my heart. I was soon in contact with a cheerful voice in the *new* shoe department. That's right! The young lady had just started two weeks ago. One of her main responsibilities was in the shoe department.

"We always have too many shoes," she informed me. "I am so glad you called. Come see me on Wednesday at nine."

*****

The beaming smile drew me right in as I met the young lady at the door. "It's the kindness of others that believe in Jesus Christ or their heavenly Father that pulls me toward believing too," the young lady offered with a smile.

Her arms were brightly colored with tattoos from shoulders to wrists. Her smile beamed with the hope and excitement that I was showing her such gratitude for helping me with my shoe collection.

"Soles 4 Souls—such a neat name," she added. "I am so glad you called me and that I could do something that makes me feel good. It makes me happy to have someone ask of me. I feel like an outcast when everyone seems to walk on by." The young lady grabbed my hand and shook it with great enthusiasm. I don't think I have had so much conversation in five minutes with anyone, let alone a stranger.

There were about 125 pairs—sweet.

"I will have a lot more for you by Friday." The young lady responded. I think I could do that much every week—if you could come to get them.

"What if I am only collecting them until the end of June?" I asked.

"Well"—she paused—"I guess someone is going barefoot."

"When God blesses a hundredfold, I guess it's true," I added.

She smiled. "What does that mean?" the young lady asked.

"If you give a little with love and truth from your heart and do it in secret, your Father in heaven will bless you many times over openly. This is all you, my young friend," I offered.

The young lady could hardly stand still with the excitement wanting to get out. "I think I am just going to love this job." She smiled. "Please take my cell number in case we can help each other. She offered a generous hug and smiled. She offered an "it's so nice to be appreciated" as we departed. I never thought this was going to be a help-each-other situation. I never thought it was a witness opportunity. I never thought it would be a request for friendship. I never thought it would be more than trying to pick up a few pairs of shoes. I surely wouldn't be able to get more than getting maybe ten pairs of shoes. Ten pairs would be good, right?

> But thou, when thou prayest, enter into thy closet, and when thou hast shut thy door, pray to thy Father which is in secret; and thy Father which seeth in secret shall reward thee openly. (Matthew 6:6)

So now my cup runs over because I have more shoes than I know what to do with. My young friend thought she will have another good amount for next week. I was told we will start a new one thing a week early but still take shoes next week. I wish I had some storage for shoes. Even the smallest word or deed done in God's will creates tremendous results.

I have to go into this testimony and add a small portion. While reflecting this story to a couple of young ladies this week, they became enthused and collected a large number of shoes from their closets. It didn't take but a split few seconds for them to want to help. There was a lot of love in those two hearts, God bless them. One young lady was the daughter of the other and was getting ready to celebrate her twelfth birthday. She excitedly exclaimed that she would have her friends bring shoes for her gifts so she could give them to Soles4Soles. I know why Jesus likes young people so well. They have unconditional love! Bless them and keep them, Father! That's amazing!

I returned on Friday to pick up some more shoes. I had more than I could hardly haul in my pickup. I had to make a delivery to the church. There were more than five hundred pairs of shoes. The crate was now more than full, and my young friend had asked me to come back next week. I returned the following Wednesday to pick up three hundred pairs, which I put in my garage. On Friday I picked up over two hundred more pairs of shoes. I thought I should call the church before I brought the shoes over. A nice young lady answered the phone, and I informed her I had over five hundred pairs of shoes to deliver to the church.

"Oh, please don't bring any more shoes. We are too full!"

My heart sank to the floor. I sat on the back of my pickup and looked at the big load of shoes. I felt like I was out of breath, but I prayed. "Father, I humbly come before thy throne. Whisper, I pray, thy words of wisdom. Show me the path for these shoes?"

Immediately an answer came to me. "Seek the stranger that feeds my people."

Feeds my people! *Feeds my people*, I thought. I thought about calling Faith Temple church, but then I thought about the Banquet. I called the Banquet and spoke with Tamara, the director. I didn't know her, but she was very nice.

"We don't really do a giveaway like shoes. I will talk about it and get back tomorrow," she directed.

The next day, I spoke with Tamara, and she informed me they would try a shoe giveaway as a one-time thing.

"Would I have any children's shoes?" she asked.

"I haven't seen many children's shoes in what I had received so far," I replied. "You don't know what you will get until the boxes are opened," I added.

"We will still do it," Tamara informed as she hung up.

I went to the Banquet address at the requested time for delivery. As I had just finished backing up to the door, a young lady appeared.

"Hi, are you Tamara, by any chance?" I asked.

"Yes, I am," she replied.

"Nice to meet you," I replied as I stretched out my hand. "Do you believe in prayer?" I asked boldly.

"Yes, I do," Tamara replied.

"Well, Father in heaven, let there be children's shoes in these boxes?" I asked.

We unloaded the boxes and started opening them up. There were so many boxes of children's shoes I could have just cried for joy. It was no doubt a very pleasant surprise to Tamara.

I asked Tamara, "Where would be a good place to call for more shoe placement?"

She quickly replied, "Pastor Hayes at the Faith Temple church."

Very quickly I thought about the prayer of seeking out the stranger that feeds my people. I called Pastor Hayes and asked if I could give shoes out at his food giveaway at the fairgrounds.

"We have never done this before, but I think it would be a good idea," he responded with enthusiasm.

I collected the shoes for the following week and informed Pastor Hayes that I would have over a pickup load which would be well over five hundred pairs of shoes.

On Friday, we arrived at the fairgrounds with Lindy and a young new enthusiastic friend, Jordynn. We marked and sorted shoes onto a dozen tables, which Pastor Hayes had provided. It was almost two when we finished preparing shoes. Many, many people were forming in a line to wait.

"Come and have shoes as many as you need," I called out with a motion of my arm.

They came and they came as we directed people to the various sizes.

A middle-aged man came to me and asked, "Would you have any shoes for me?" He asked almost as a plea.

I looked at his tennis shoes, which still reflect the colors of a rainbow. They were beyond being worn out, to say the least.

"Let's go down to the last table, where there are a few larger pairs."

We were almost at the table when his pace quickened. There was one pair of size 13 tennis shoes sitting in the middle of the table. He grabbed up the shoes and hugged them to his face. They looked almost new—and guess what? They were a shoe of many colors! He smiled at me with great joy as he ran to an old car to sit down and put the shoes on.

"Father in heaven, who needs joy from anything else when we have you?"

Love in Christ, Fred

Love Is in the Air

September 2013

Thought: A letter for you with as much love as it can carry. May the Spirit of God direct you in all ways, this I pray! Let's have a testimonial story and see what we can learn about walking with strangers, possible angels, and not being embarrassed about what you are compelled to do.

To all with love,

I was ever so grateful to have a job. When you feel this way, it makes you happy. Oh, I am sure there are tasks in all jobs that just don't cut it. A nice fellow by the name of Gary gave me a job, for which I really didn't have experience, working in a hardware store in Jackson, Minnesota. I will always be thankful for this time, as we all should.

On this particular day in mid-February, there was a fierce snow-storm in the making. I only refer to a snowstorm as being fierce when the wind brings along a white-out condition with severe wind chills. The snow had been falling all day, and as early afternoon came about, the wind was picking up. Gary, the owner of the store, came up to me when he came back from lunch.

"It's getting bad out there," he spoke seriously. "You may want to go home early. It's okay by me. There is hardly anyone around."

"It's fine with me, Gary. It's nearly three. I would like to get home before dark. My little Toyota isn't the best in snow," I replied.

I saluted Gary. "Good day, and I will see you tomorrow." I punched out, grabbed my coat, and was soon visiting my rusty little orange pickup. The snow I was walking in seemed to be six or seven inches deep. The vehicle started right off, and in a couple of minutes, it was warmed up.

As I started down the street, I could feel the little pickup pushing through the snow. It was deep enough for sure. I waited at the stoplight and observed how fast I had to turn the wipers on to get the snow to clear. I looked up and down the streets as I passed them, heading out of town toward the interstate. As I climbed up the long rolling hill, the wind seemed to escalate. The closer I got toward the interstate, the greater the white-out condition grew.

I soon found the ramp to enter the interstate, and because of the poor conditions, I kept looking in the mirror and over my shoulder to see if there were any vehicles coming. All of a sudden, I saw someone standing at the top of the ramp. I passed by due to the reaction time. I looked out the back window to make sure I saw what I saw. I paused there with disbelief. You would surely freeze to death if you were out here in these conditions. Soon the to-be passenger opened the door.

"Please get in before you freeze," I encouraged the stranger. "Where are you going?"

"Wherever you are going," was his response.

"I live in the next town. It's only about fifteen miles further down the interstate. How long have you been standing at the top of the entrance ramp?" I further inquired.

"A while," he replied softly.

"Don't you have gloves or a hat? You could easily freeze out there," I continued as I turned the heater up to full on.

He gave no response. I headed the little pickup out onto the interstate.

"It's going to be slow and a little difficult going," I offered, which was obvious. I saw his tattered coat. He had no gloves and no hat. His coat was something you would wear in fall. His beard was full, and his hair was to his shoulders. He sat there motionless and stared out the windshield, as I did, searching for the road.

"Is there anything I can do for you?" I asked maybe just to break the silence.

"You are doing it," the stranger replied in his soft voice.

"I mean something more than just this ride. Where are you trying to get to?" I offered.

"Just east," he replied in his soft voice. "I have all I need," he continued a moment later.

I looked slightly in his direction when he responded. My eyes caught the sight of my gloves beside me on the seat. There were a few small holes in them, but he had none. I wonder if he would be embarrassed if I offered them to him. I felt sorry for him though I wouldn't say. I wrestled with the idea of giving him something.

I would like to take him home for some super, but my wife would never have that: "Never bring a stranger home. We have little children here."

That wouldn't go well, but what could I do? I had one winter coat. *Could I give him my coat?* I thought.

We continued on down the road in silence. There were no vehicles going either way. I couldn't leave him out on the interstate as I had found him.

"I am going to take you into town when we get there. There is a Casey's store just off the interstate. You can be warm and wait for a possible ride."

"It doesn't look as if anyone is even out here. Would this be all right?"

"I don't know where else you would be safe," I instructed.

The stranger said, "That's fine." He said no more as we continued.

"I see a landmark. We are almost there," I stated.

There was no response. I thought about giving the stranger some money, but I wasn't sure if I had any. I think I had given my wife what I had that morning for groceries.

We crept off the interstate and started into town. There wasn't a soul in sight. I pulled into Casey's. There still wasn't anyone around. I pulled up close to the front of the store so I could see if anyone was inside. I saw someone standing by the front counter.

"You should be okay here. Good luck," I encouraged.

"Thank you," the stranger responded as he exited the pickup.

When he closed the door, I started to pull away. Rather than going to the street, I drove around the pumps and came back to the front of the store where I had let the stranger out. I was taking him home for a meal at least. I would pay my dues if they came my way. That would be the least I could do.

He wasn't standing there, so I got out and went into the store. I had to pull extra hard to get the store door open. I stepped in almost out of breath. I saw Dale standing behind the counter. I viewed around the store.

"Hi, Dale, where is the young man I just let out of my pickup?" I asked Dale.

"There has been no one in the store for over an hour," he replied. "I have been standing right here for fifteen minutes."

"Really?" I questioned as I returned out the door.

> For there stood by me this night the angel
> of God, whose I am, and whom I serve. (Acts
> 27:23)

I hurried back outside. I looked around the corner of the store. I hurried back to the pickup and went around the street. I saw nothing. I went back around the store to see if the stranger had gone to the backside of the building. I drove back toward the interstate—no one. I was perplexed as I started for home.

While mentioning the travels home with the stranger, my wife gave a response that he must have been crazy to be out in a storm like this. "Good thing you didn't bring him home with you." I didn't mention that I was going to. The story suddenly stopped there, but I couldn't get the stranger out of my head.

> Be not forgetful to entertain strangers: for
> thereby some have entertained angels unawares.
> (Hebrews 13:2)

The next day it was back to work. I was up at four and started scooping out the driveway. It was an hour-and-a-half snow removal. The plows were out, and most of the primary roads were open. I knew I had to get to the store early to clear the snow out around the store. It was work as usual, and having put yesterday behind, it seemed like a normal day. It was midafternoon when I heard one of my coworkers page me from the front of the store.

"Fred, there is someone here to see you."

I was in the far back corner of the store. I walked to the main aisle so I could quickly see who it was. I didn't recognize the person as I walked up the aisle. The individual walked quickly toward me. It was a taller man with a thick black beard and black hair. He was very nicely dressed, with a long black overcoat. When he was still about ten feet away, he reached his hand out with a very nice pair of gloves.

"These gloves are yours," the stranger offered in a loud voice.

My first reaction was to reach my hand out, but then I pulled it back and replied, "No, they are not mine."

"Yes, please take them!" the stranger insisted in a controlling voice.

My hand was about halfway up when the gloves were thrust into my hand. He did an about-face and briskly went toward the front of the store. I quickly reflected on my holey gloves that lay beside me in the pickup yesterday. I wanted to give them to the stranger yesterday. I was dumbfounded. I looked up to see the stranger reach the front door. I ran to the front of the store and rushed outside. I looked both ways and ran to the corner of the store to look around the corner. There was no one to be seen. I quickly went back to the corner and frantically looked everywhere.

Father in heaven, fill my soul. Let me not be a broken soul. Many, many times in my life you have sent a messenger. May every breath I take give you glory. Thoughts rushed through my mind.

> Are they not all ministering spirits, sent
> forth to minister for them who shall be heirs of
> salvation? (Hebrews 1:14)

I returned to the store and asked Joanne if she knew who the gentleman was that had just been in the store. Her response was, "I have never seen him before.

"He was very direct and gave me these gloves," I replied. "He said these were mine, but I assured him they were not. He practically put them in my pocket."

I slowly walked to the back of the store as I examined the gloves. They were fur-lined, black leather. And as I pulled them on, they fit like a glove. They were double stitched. They were new and smelled new. I walked over to my coat and went to put the gloves in my coat pocket. I had to pull out my old ones. I dropped one, and I saw the holes as I picked it up. I put the old ones in one pocket and the new ones in the other. It brought tears to my eyes. I swallowed hard and walked to the back corner of the store so no one could see my tears. *Someone loves me*, I thought. My God, whose name is, I Am, loves me.

> Likewise, I say unto you, there is joy in the presence of the angels of God over one sinner that repented. (Luke 15:10)

Love in Christ, Fred

Silver Coin of Truth

October 2013

Thought: A letter for you with as much love as it can carry. May the Spirit of God direct you in all ways, this I pray! Let's have a testimonial story about a whisper from the Holy Spirit. You will know right away! When you know it's the Holy Spirit, do what is requested.

To all with love,

The silver coin of truth is one of ten coins we sent out. The coin itself is the most highly refined coin ever minted in the world. Its value is actually $4 to $5 more than the price of silver. Right now that would be about $26. The point is not that, however. The point is that the word of Jesus Christ our Lord is more refined and full of truth than silver refined seven times in the ground. When you look upon or touch the coin, please think of the truth of Christ.

> That thine alms may be in secret: and thy Father which seeth in secret himself shall reward thee openly. (Matthew 6:4)

> The words of the LORD are pure words: as silver tried in a furnace of earth, purified seven times. (Psalm 12:6)

When we were asked to pray for three strangers who were physically upon their deathbed, we prayed immediately. All three are alive today and doing very well, praise be to my Father in heaven. This was the first week. In week two we were asked to pray for seven others in serious pain, illness, and loss. Each person came to us by someone else. The pain, loss, and illness were very real. We prayed immediately! The letters and gifts would follow. The gifts sent with each letter were also requested by the Holy Spirit. I never really knew why I kept these strange gifts, but each of you received the one meant for each of you. I just happened to have just seven of the gifts. I found that interesting when I went looking for them. *The strangest gifts ever*, I thought. I am happy to report that each had received great strength or is overcoming their illness, all by the hand of the Holy Spirit and nothing that I could ever do. All but one were strangers. Our love for each is as real as we consider them family. Be of strength and courage. We have been blessed very greatly over this service to the Lord.

I believe in prayer, answers to prayer through faith, and salvation in Jesus Christ. The answers to prayers come in all forms; just wait quietly and patiently in faith.

A particular scripture I read one night and then prayed was of the truth of Christ. After about an hour, a stranger of some form appeared in the doorway. I was struck with a fear that seemed to melt me. It whispered to my mind to send forth the ten silver coins of truth.

"Messenger, is that you?" I whispered.

I prepared to lunge forward to catch hold of the being. In a flash, my arm was hit with a burning sensation. I cried for a bit and rested until my strength came back to me. These types of events have been a part of my life since I was eight. They still scare me and fill me with joy. I do understand why the majority can't believe these events. I too question them, pray about them, and seek what service I can do for my Lord.

> But thou, when thou prayest, enter into thy closet, and when thou hast shut thy door, pray to thy Father which is in secret; and thy Father which seeth in secret shall reward thee openly. (Matthew 6:6)

Again I say unto you, that if two of you shall
agree on earth as touching anything that they
shall ask, it shall be done for them of my Father
which is in heaven. (Matthew 18:19)

I then prayed for forgiveness for trying such a foolish thing.
Also, in the prayer, I asked as to where I should get the money to
buy the coins and what these coins might be. The next day, a letter
arrived and requested me to put my money market monies in a different account. I have no such account! I just left it for three days
when Linda thought she would go searching. In a short time, she
found an account which we had closed four years ago.

"Hey mister, with pennies in an account, how about multiply-
ing that times a thousand?"

Long story short is that 10 percent of this amount equaled the
value of the ten coins. Linda gave a wow, and I gave a praise of glory
to the Father. God gives me fear and joy at the same time.

We quickly dropped all things and went to a small coin dealer
to ask about the purest silver coins available. When he spoke of the
American silver dollar and its purification seven times, we bought the
ten coins. We quickly sent out the coins without delay.

Not all believe in prayer, the answers to prayer, or in salvation
or in the one and only way to salvation through Jesus Christ. These
coins will no doubt mean something different to each receiver. I only
do what I am asked. The Holy Spirit will do the real work. My life is
so different the last four years, but Jesus Christ is so real.

When some beings called me the little lion who would not roar,
the one who walks the dusty road, and the child of the lost generation, it made me sad, empty, and then a little bold. I requested the
beings to depart from me, for I serve only the Son of God who sits
on the right hand of his Father. They proclaimed their service to the
ancient of days. I became very afraid and melted to the ground or
whatever was under me.

"Is the dusty road the road I walked for a mile and drove almost
a thousand miles to do and praise my Father?" I asked.

They confirmed it as so and that it was also some fifty years ago. It was the bread I had given to a stranger some fifty years ago as I had walked that same piece of road. I burst into tears of shame, joy, and of things so much more awesome than I could ever imagine. Why had I done it was the question.

"I am a child now and was a child then," I confessed.

When a messenger first told me a stranger would arrive in three days to guide me, I cannot disbelieve Pastor Vernon Peterson was that person. I am forever grateful for his love and guidance. He is clearly the most devoted person I have ever met. He told me many times that I would fall, but always—but always go to the cross. Always gaze upon God and blink at life. Other things happened, but it's a lot to wrap your head around.

I have a tendency to analyze everything. I would still like to know how a flash of light sent me to talk to these messengers of God, how they know everything about us even unto years and years before we are born. One simple thing in one day that we do for our Lord becomes a monumental moment. May we listen ever intently for the voice of our Lord. We all will fall but rush back to the cross of salvation. Don't expect rewards and blessings as some payment. Let our Father be who he is and just be all you can be. I have seen blessings come back to me greater than I could imagine. Your Father in heaven knows when it's right to bless and when to chastise. There is a certain season, you know.

> To everything there is a season, and a time to every purpose under the heaven: A time to be born, and a time to die; a time to plant, and a time to pluck up that which is planted; a time to kill, and a time to heal; a time to break down, and a time to build up; a time to weep, and a time to laugh; a time to mourn, and a time to dance; a time to cast away stones, and a time to gather stones together; a time to embrace, and a time to refrain from embracing; a time to get, and a time to lose; a time to keep, and a time to cast

away; a time to rend, and a time to sew; a time to keep silence, and a time to speak; a time to love, and a time to hate; a time of war, and a time of peace. What profit hath he that worketh in that wherein he laboureth? (Ecclesiastes 3:1–9)

Love in Christ, Fred

The Power of Prayer

November 2013

Thought: A letter for you with as much love as it can carry. May the Spirit of God direct you in all ways, this I pray! Let's have a testimonial story and see what we can learn about prayer.

To all with love,

Please believe that you can have a personal, intimate conversation with your savior every day. Get close! Prayer is a conversation with *God*—the intercourse of the soul with *God*, not in contemplation or meditation but in direct address to him. Prayer may be oral or mental, occasional or constant, ejaculatory or formal. It is a "beseeching the *Lord*" (Exodus 32:11); "pouring out the soul before the Lord" (1 Samuel 1:15); "praying and crying to *heaven*" (2 Chronicles 32:20); "seeking unto *God* and making supplication" (Job 8:5); "drawing near to *God*" (Psalm 73:28); "*bowing* the knees" (Ephesians 3:14).

It's November, and I'm standing in the driveway of the project house we are working on. Father, hold back the frigid temperatures so that I may finish the concrete paving in this driveway. I am on a waiting list for a contractor to show up. Perhaps if I was a little younger, I would just get at it. I walked around, picking up the area as I gave my Father praise for the beauty of the day. A gaze down the street revealed all the trees empty of leaves. *To everything there is a season*, I thought. I noticed one tree across the street and up one house which still had all its leaves. It looked like a maple, but the leaves seemed very large. It was a beautiful tree. May the beauty of Jesus be in your heart even when all else seems desolate. Many people would just look on by that tree and give a shrug. I thought of it as beautiful and dynamic in the creation of God.

> And he said unto them, When ye pray, say, "Our Father which art in heaven, Hallowed be thy name. Thy kingdom come, Thy will be done, as in heaven, so in earth. Give us day by day our daily bread. And forgive us our sins; for we also forgive every one that is indebted to us. And lead us not into temptation; but deliver us from evil." (Luke 11:2–4)

I continued the cleaning around the backyard and the clinging of the frost on the items I was picking up. First one trip then back for another load of misplaced debris. I again came around the corner of the house and delivered my items to the pile. I suddenly stopped. I had to check to make sure my mouth wasn't hanging open as I stood staring at the colorful tree across the street. The leaves were raining down off the beautiful tree. It was very quiet out, no sounds, no people. You could almost hear the leaves as they seem to pile up under the tree. A silver van drove past me and stopped at a mailbox. I hardly paid any attention to it as I was intrigued by the tree.

What a climax, I thought. I had never seen this dropping of the leaves from a tree like this. First, they are all there in the beauty of the tree in fall, and then in a dynamic fashion, they all start releasing.

A middle-aged lady in the silver van drove across the street and got out of the van in the drive. I waved and apologized for staring at her tree. She waved back, so I thought I would walk across the street for a minute. It was Sharron. I had met her a few days earlier. She had just lost her husband a short time ago.

We stood in the falling leaves.

"You have a beautiful, magical tree in your yard," I commented.

"Thanks. I received this tree when I was in sixth grade from my science teacher," Sharron offered. "My sister got the one in the backyard. Her tree is a cranapple. My husband and I would laugh at the birds that would get drunk off the berries that would fall to the ground and ferment. This tree, I think, is called a Russian maple."

"It seems like this tree is going to drop all of its leaves today?" I questioned.

"It will!" Sharron informed me. "They will all be gone by dark or sooner. It has always been the last to drop but the very quickest to drop."

"It is a very mysterious tree," I replied. It's like the mysteries of God being revealed. The secrets of our Father in heaven are limitless. This very tree has a purpose even if today it's a few words for us to share. I don't take prayer lightly, Sharron, and I will pray for you."

"Thanks for stopping for a visit," Sharron offered in appreciation. "I feel a little closer to God today."

It was an appreciated conversation as we parted. A few small words of God and his hands on all things seemed to leave strength to both of us. Give a word, and get a moment.

I went back to work but couldn't help myself but to give my Father the glory for the moment, for the strength that seemed to flow into Sharron. Every moment, every breath is a gift from God. You have to want to see and believe. Step into the light.

The thoughts of giving Jesus glory and praises bombarded me as I worked through the day. Upon leaving and driving home, I began to praise God. I often like to give my Father glory and praise as I travel. I suddenly stopped in frustration and shouted out that this was just noise. It was sometimes like at church when you just feel its noise. The burst of frustration surprised me. I implored my Father to give me an understanding of him, of praise and prayer. I then became apologetic as I tried to give glory to God for the day. I became so emotional I couldn't speak. All suddenly became still and quiet. I thought I heard a voice ask me to "seek the prophet Enoch."

The name Enoch—what? I had to think as to where I had heard the name before. I didn't know much about Enoch but that he was in the Bible. I don't know when the last time I ever said the name

Enoch—forever, I guess! Where did this come from? I wanted to talk to my Jesus, not Enoch.

I went searching when I got home. "Father, I probably do not know what I am asking. Please show me the words which you gave to Enoch that I may be filled."

Enoch was the seventh generation from Adam. He was the great grandfather of Noah. I searched through the Bible for a few bits concerning the prophet Enoch. I didn't seem to be getting an answer to my questions. My head was filling up with more questions than I had before. My biggest question was whether or not I was going to continue with my first testimony letters into the next year. Just for the fun of it, I asked Google for "the word of Enoch. It suddenly appeared—the word of God as it was given to Enoch. I never knew this existed. So the whisper of my Father in heaven is true, as always, again. Seek the words of Enoch, and I shall have my questions answered. I tremble in the fear and awesomeness of God, yet I rejoice in it also. So my life goes in a hundred directions; I will pray a thousand prayers to go in the correct path.

I have found myself praising God more in prayer, praising his holiness, humbling myself, and always asking for his mercy. I think we take prayer too lightly. We need to find the prayer closet and get serious. It may seem a bit difficult to pray for an hour or perhaps two. I think that prayer needs to claim the holiness of our Lord, to extol his being, and to humble ourselves before the throne of God. Until I was directed to find the word of Enoch, I never knew there were angels that prepare our prayers unto the Father. I never knew that the angels served our holy Father so diligently. I never knew that each person was so important to the angels. We are so important to them because our Lord Jesus Christ is so merciful to us. The angels serve the Father so intently because of his love and holiness.

Our Father cherishes us so dearly. Why, one of the great commandments asks us to honor our father and mother is because of the one and only person we are, that only our father and mother at a given point in time have allowed us to be here. Try to wrap your head around the value of the most precious jewel in the world and the value of it. Take yourself and multiply it times a thousand times ten thousand and ten thousand. The value is higher than I can comprehend. Get the picture?

After praying for about thirty minutes, I had a flash of light in my mind. It was unusual for me as I have never experienced this before. It has only been in the last year that I have prayed fairly long prayers of praise and emotion. I immediately was standing in the presence of several large shadows.

I asked the question, "What are you, large shadows, which I see in this vision?"

The great shadows replied, "We are they that serve."

I asked, "Can I look upon you?"

The shadows replied, "No, we are not permitted."

I became fearful and fell on my face. "I give glory to the holy one whom you serve," I whispered.

This is more than my understanding. My praise and glory are to Jesus Christ, my Lord and savior.

"What is this place?"

"This is a place where the spirit reaches prayer to the holy one," a voice instructed. "The spirit of God is the great comforter."

"You are of the lost generation," a voice spoke.

Another said, "You are the lion who would not be a lion. Roar, little lion."

Another voice replied, "This is the one who walks the dusty road."

"How do you know that?" I asked.

"We know all things through the wisdom the holy one gives us. Ask what you will?"

"How may I find a way to walk upon the path of righteousness?" I asked. "Let that portion of the Holy Spirit come upon me which I may serve my Savior?"

"Go into the way that you have chosen," one of the great shadows spoke. It is the desire of the Father that all would pray in the spirit. It is not the length of the prayer but of faith, love, and devotion. Many words are given to prayer but lack the spirit. As you have been instructed earlier, all of heaven rejoices over one who surrenders to the son of God. It is not your requirement in service to bear responsibility that all should accept the son of God as their savior. Many shall reject, and only few will accept."

"I can't comprehend your devotion," I replied.

I have had no relatives commit to the Word of God, so my instruction has been given to me by strangers sent by the hand of my Father in heaven. I give my Father praise for each breath I have. I am so very thankful for each stranger sent into my life. Holy, holy, holy is the Great I Am.

A breath blew over me and instructed me with a firm voice, "Look through the parting in the shadows. Testify the way you found the kingdom of the Most High. Roar, little lion."

I saw an untold number of people falling into a great, black canyon.

"Don't go into the black canyon!" I shouted. "Call upon the son of God and be saved!" I roared with all my strength.

They wouldn't stop, and I fell on my face and cried. I arose; my face was wet, and so I dried my face. It was as if a switch had been flipped. I tried to wrap my head around this vision. *Wow*, I thought. Unfortunately, in the past when I came close to God, I would run away in fear. I would have visions and requests of me. They would seem so tremendous. I wouldn't share because I feared the awesomeness of God. I always thought I would say the wrong thing.

When one person, only one, accepts Jesus Christ as their savior, the heavens ring with joy from the multitude of angels. Wow! So for me, to ask the question as to whether or not I should share a testimonial each month is a resounding yes! I shall roar as the little lion. I shall roar as I had found the kingdom of God. I shall bow ever more humbly unto the throne of my Savior. This is way over my head but exciting.

The next day, a middle-aged lady came up to me and thanked me for sharing my testimonials. She asked, hopefully, that I would continue. She reflected that she went to church occasionally but never felt committed. She laid her hand on my arm and started to cry. I have never thought of God as being with me daily. I just thought he was like out there somewhere. She burst into a rain of emotion. I gave her a hug and told her to "believe as in the faith of a child.

Believe that every breath is a gift of God. Glorify and exalt the name of our Lord and savior, for it is right to do."

At that moment, I was compassionate for all the children of God. How much more our Father must feel.

> Then thou scarest me with dreams, and terrifiest me through visions. (Job 7:14)

> And it shall come to pass afterward, *that* I will pour out my spirit upon all flesh; and your sons and your daughters shall prophesy, your old men shall dream dreams, your young men shall see visions. (Joel 2:28)

> I Daniel was grieved in my spirit in the midst of *my* body, and the visions of my head troubled me. (Daniel 7:15)

> And it shall come to pass in the last days, saith God, "I will pour out of my Spirit upon all flesh: and your sons and your daughters shall prophesy, and your young men shall see visions, and your old men shall dream dreams." (Acts 2:17)

> And when he had taken the book, the four beasts and four *and* twenty elders fell down before the Lamb, having every one of them harps, and golden vials full of odours, which are the prayers of saints. (Revelation 5:8)

> Confess *your* faults one to another, and pray one for another, that ye may be healed. The effectual fervent prayer of a righteous man availeth much. (James 5:16)

And when he looked on him, he was afraid, and said, "What is it, Lord?" And he said unto him, "Thy prayers and thine alms are come up for a memorial before God." (Acts 10:4)

Be careful for nothing; but in everything by prayer and supplication with thanksgiving let your requests be made known unto God. (Philippians 4:6)

And all things, whatsoever ye shall ask in prayer, believing, ye shall receive. (Matthew 21:22)

So why is there a conflict? When I take on a new mission for God, I get blasted for the effort. Here it comes! I always get a bit uneasy because Satan goes about seeking whom he may destroy. I was to take someone out for lunch, by request, as he wanted to show me something and discuss something. So we did, and the first thing he showed me was when he threw his arm upon the table. He is a big guy and, thus, a big arm.

"What do you think?" the man requested.

"Is that a bat?" I asked.

"It's a gargoyle," he responded with a laugh.

"It's nasty, and a waste," I replied.

"It's a myth, like your God and testimonies." The man laughed. "Look at the little cherubim it is crushing in its claws," he added.

"Are you asking for a death wish?" I asked. "You can't get rid of it now."

"Oh, I could have it removed if I wanted." He laughed again.

"It's in your heart, your mind, and your soul," I spoke sternly back to him. "Not just on your arm. Jesus Christ is the only one that can get that out of you."

The middle-aged man suddenly got very serious and quiet.

"I am very disappointed in you, but I will pray for you."

The next week, I went over to a project house we had finished just to check on it. It had been about a week since we were there and cleaned it. I went in thru the garage door. I tried to open the door to the kitchen, but it was severely jammed shut and crooked. The latch was totally loose. I hit it hard with my shoulder a couple of times before it opened. All of the interior doors were like this. The rolling closet doors were also off their tracks. I called the contractor who had done the basement wall corrections. He soon arrived with his brother. They examined walls, windows, floors, and ceilings. They leveled and measured every surface for about forty minutes. They discussed many things in disbelief. We stood there discussing many things.

"We have no idea," the contractor insisted. "We see it but don't believe what we are seeing," they added together as they looked at each other.

"Maybe it's the hand of God allowing this?" I questioned.

They both suddenly looked at me and replied together, "We have to go." They quickly walked away and added, "Sorry for your mischief. Wait for it."

The next week, a very elderly lady I help from time to time met me in the hallway. We greeted each other.

"Please don't send me your monthly letters anymore," she requested. "I don't believe in God as part of your life like you do."

"As you wish," I responded as she seemed to quickly walk away.

She reminded me of aunts and uncles, which just never wanted me to speak about God. I have had many family members just say it's silly. I have been very privileged to say to some folks that God is going to do something for you—and he does. They are amazed but quickly forget. Why bother? The vast majority of people don't believe in God truly answering prayers. God grieves in his heart for the love lost. He wants his children to come to him. He has done everything to save his children including the offering of Jesus Christ on the cross of salvation.

I had to do some serious praying. I didn't like the pattern of events, which were appearing. "Father, turn not thy head aside. Only you are holy and worthy of glory. I am but sin but plead for thy mercy. I shall not turn aside from you. Cast me aside if you wish, or guard me against that which I cannot see. I humbly come before your throne."

After about a half hour of praying, I suddenly saw the great black canyon which I had seen once before. I again saw the great multitude of people falling into the blackness. They were silent before, but this time they were screaming. I had to put my hands over my ears.

"Knock the dust from your shoes if the Word is not received," a voice instructed. "Roar, little lion."

I again arose as before and dried my face. I sat wondering if people who pray with great intent have such conclusions as this. The vision was more intent, and the sound still rings in my mind. There was a point trying to be made even if it was of great sadness.

Ask in prayer

Ask, and it will be given to you seek, and you will find; knock, and it will be opened to you. (Matthew 7:7)

And whatever you ask in prayer, you will receive, if you have faith. (Matthew 21:22)

Therefore I tell you, whatever you ask in prayer, believe that you have received it, and it will be yours. (Mark 11:24)

Whatever you ask in my name, this I will do, that the Father may be glorified in the Son. If you ask me anything in my name, I will do it. (John 14:13–14)

What Season Is It?

December 2013

Thought: A letter for you with as much love as it can carry. May the Spirit of God direct you in all ways, this I pray! To all with love, let's have a testimonial story about when you pray, follow through with what is asked of you by the Holy Spirit. One doesn't challenge God, but the question by a young lady was to show her where I thought God helped me every day for the next week. Let's see!

To all with love,

The other day, a question came up as to if God reveals his answers to prayers, his hopes for us, his blessings, and his protection at just certain times. Is it possible to see or hear God every day without just saying look at nature? My first response was to read the third chapter of Ecclesiastes in the Bible.

The person with questions asked, "What about something more personal?"

I was led by the Holy Spirit to give an accounting of the previous week on a daily basis. So at that moment in time, the previous week made more sense than ever to me. I immediately felt like I was hit with a ball of wind that flooded me with emotion. This, in turn, will be the first testimony story of the month. God is alive! Listen!

Sunday

By request, we had been praying about giving an additional amount to church. One gives to several needy causes, and as a rule, a Christian likes to give 10 percent of the first of your fruits of labor. The decision was to give a considerable amount to the new request. It started right away on Sunday. The answer came from God. The bank account said no! The business said no! My human nature said no because it felt like I was giving to a building and not to the people. We would wait quietly to see the result. When you feel God asked, you just do. It really was about treasures for heaven and not on this earth.

Monday

I drove to my project site and got out of the pickup. I walked around the pickup to go to the front door and unlock it. Not to the side but directly in front of me was a dead bird. It was lying on its breast, wings folded in and beak resting on its breast. It looked like it had died very peacefully. I whispered out loud, "Father, you see and know all things. My Lord and savior, please forgive me for that sin I commit, which I do not know."

This felt different from all the other birds I have seen dead over the years. The previous Monday I had a bird of a different kind directly in my path as I was taking out the trash before going to work. It too was dead in this same peaceable manner. I said then as I had said now, "Father, you see and know all things. I am sure many would say it's just two dead birds in two weeks on Mondays. No, this was the third Monday I had found a dead bird in this very manner. On the Monday previous to the last, I had walked into the backyard of the project house to pick up some tree branches. This was the third bird of a different kind that died in the same peaceable manner. I gave it no thought and just disposed of it. I was very happy that I didn't find the fourth bird on Monday of this week.

Let yourself have God in your heart, mind, soul, and your spirit—then wait! A sequence had happened that I would never forget. This was three birds, three weeks on three Mondays. I have to add to this piece because this fourth week I left the door of the project house open to air it out. A male bright-red cardinal flew into the house and spent most of the day with us singing and flying about. The cardinal was not anxious about anything but just sang and tweeted at leisure. It was time to leave, so I walked into the living room where it was sitting on the ceiling fan and tweeting. I told the cardinal it was time to go so as not to be left in the house. It flew to the dining room and the kitchen, and it sat on the top cabinet after tweeting a couple of times. Then it flew out the door. The whole thing sounded and felt inviting. I asked God to clear my head and ears that I should not miss anything he wanted me to know. Father, be merciful to the bird population.

Tuesday

My plumber friend stopped by and looked at the job he had quoted for $3,700. The job had been looked at, and the quote had been done, but out of the blue he told me he could do the job like this and that and save us $1,000. The job was done and saved $1,000. I never asked for it but gave God the glory. He had never before altered a quote he had given us.

I replied, "Let God have the glory."

He replied, "Always!"

God had rewarded a gift by manifold over what we had given.

Wednesday

I have a contractor that helps us do our roof repairs on a regular basis. He was going to stop by and pick up some scraps he had left in a pile after doing the roof last week. I helped him load the debris and went to my pickup to get the checkbook to pay him for the job. He presented the bill to me, and it was $500 less than I thought it would be. He had just printed it out in his pickup as he has a computer and printer in the truck.

"Are you sure this is right?" I asked.

"Yes, I am going to give you a discount," he replied.

"Why?" I asked. I scratched my head, perplexed.

"Business is good," he replied.

"Praise God, and thank you." I smiled.

"Praise him every day," he responded.

Linda and I laughed as we discussed what God had given us—an amount over what we were going to give as extra for the year. It happened in a three-day period.

Thursday

We had decided to remove a very nice vanity from the main bath. It was a five-foot unit in super shape. It would probably be an $800 unit today and perhaps more. It was listed for sale for $225 and immediately had multiple offers. The first was an offer for $200, the second was for $150. The third was for the $225, but she didn't know when she could get it. We waited to respond. The third offer called back an hour later and said she surely wanted it, but her help became unavailable. Should we wait? The question was asked, but the answer was to wait. An hour or so later, a third call came, and the lady said she had found someone down the street to help, but she didn't know when she could get to our location. A fourth call came, and a time was given to pick the vanity up. It was five o'clock when the pickup and trailer pulled into the drive.

A lady in her midthirties introduced herself as Rebecca. The driver was a kind neighbor from down the street, and the other young lady was her daughter. She was a lady with a bubbly personality. I proceeded to show them the vanity.

"It's just a lovely piece," she expressed with joy. It was sitting a short distance away.

I then pointed to the top. "It had a small wear flaw," I pointed out.

"It's beautiful," she expressed.

We are making a bathroom in the basement for my daughter. She is going to stay with us at home as she goes to college. She gave her daughter a hug with an expression of great joy. This is very heavy.

"Are you going to be able to unload this?" I asked.

"I have myself and my five daughters. We just work together to get things done. We always figure things out."

"Can I offer you anything in the garage for the rest of your remodel?" I asked. "Pick out anything you want."

"Really?" she asked with a smile.

"Here, take these faucets and fill lines," I offered. They are in very good shape.

"I don't have any more money," she insisted.

"No cost for anything you want."

Rebecca gave me a huge hug. "Thank you so much," she offered. She wiped the start of a tear away with the back of her hand. "I am so happy," Rebecca offered.

She stood a few feet away and continued to express herself as she gave a small nudge with her left elbow to her daughter. She, in turn, came over and gave me a hug and thank you.

"You are very welcome," I responded. "Please, see what you may need."

There was a bath stool I was going to reinstall, but I let them have it along with various plumbing pieces I normally use. I have great compassion for happy, grateful people.

Friday

It was late in the day, and I was tired. It was after five and a little like rain. We had worked on the sump pump the day before, and the float had not worked. A new one was purchased, and I had it with me. I walked down and looked at the sump tank. Water was slightly seeping in the tile, so the sump had to be fixed. I walked upstairs to get the parts.

"Father in heaven, you see all things. Could you make the sump pump work so I don't have to?" I asked out loud.

As I walked back down the steps, a still voice said, "Turn it upside down."

"Turn it upside down," I spoke out.

I walked to the sump and looked at it. I had moved, turned, and rattled it every way possible yesterday. Upside down, upside down it will go.

I plugged it in and turned it as much upside down as I could, and it worked. I put it back into its normal position, and it worked just fine.

I laughed. "Father, you make me laugh!" I shouted. I took the part and left for home.

Saturday

Now Sunday is a day of rest, but Saturday is most often a day of work. I had a lot of things had had to be done for carpet installation. It just seemed like plaster dried faster, paint dried faster, and every cut of trim came out just right. When things go this well, I just can't help but give my Father in heaven the praise for it. I had a friend that was going to show up at any time to pick up some things, which I give him to refurbish and sell. I had been doing this for a couple of years and knew he appreciated it all. To my surprise, he showed up and gave me a very nice bread maker. I was so pleased. He was equally pleased to see my gratitude.

"Thank God for good hearts," I expressed.

"I am starting to believe," he responded.

We had a moment, which boosted my day. He again had to shake my hand to express his love and appreciation.

Search each day, and you will find God. He may even find you first. Good things in and good things out. Bad things in, and you get bad things out. This one week was shared with someone who needed this to help believe. May this testimony help all who read this. I also suggest reading chapter 3 of Ecclesiastes:

> To every*thing there is* a season, and a time
> to every purpose under the heaven: A time to be
> born, and a time to die; a time to plant, and a
> time to pluck up *that which is* planted; a time to
> kill, and a time to heal; a time to break down, and

a time to build up; a time to weep, and a time to laugh; a time to mourn, and a time to dance; a time to cast away stones, and a time to gather stones together; a time to embrace, and a time to refrain from embracing; a time to get, and a time to lose; a time to keep, and a time to cast away; a time to rend, and a time to sew; a time to keep silence, and a time to speak; a time to love, and a time to hate; a time of war, and a time of peace. What profit hath he that worketh in that wherein he laboureth? I have seen the travail, which God hath given to the sons of men to be exercised in it. He hath made every*thing* beautiful in his time: also he hath set the world in their heart, so that no man can find out the work that God maketh from the beginning to the end. I know that *there is* no good in them, but for *a man* to rejoice, and to do good in his life. And also that every man should eat and drink, and enjoy the good of all his labour, it *is* the gift of God. I know that, whatsoever God doeth, it shall be for ever: nothing can be put to it, nor any thing taken from it: and God doeth *it*, that *men* should fear before him. That which hath been is now; and that which is to be hath already been; and God requireth that which is past. And moreover I saw under the sun the place of judgment, *that* wickedness *was* there; and the place of righteousness, *that* iniquity *was* there. I said in mine heart, God shall judge the righteous and the wicked: for *there is* a time there for every purpose and for every work. I said in mine heart concerning the estate of the sons of men that God might manifest them, and that they might see that they themselves are beasts. For that which befalleth the sons of men befalleth beasts; even one thing befalleth them: as the one dieth, so dieth the other; yea, they have all one breath; so that a man hath no preeminence above a beast: for all *is* vanity. All go unto one place; all are of the dust, and all turn to dust again. Who knoweth the spirit of man that goeth upward, and the spirit of the beast that goeth downward to the earth? Wherefore I perceive that *there is* nothing better, than that a man should rejoice in his own works; for that *is* his portion: for who shall bring him to see what shall be after him? (Ecclesiastes 3:1–22)

Love in Christ, Fred

We Rise and Fall Together

———— ✑ ————

January 2014

Thought: A letter for you with as much love as it can carry. May the Spirit of God direct you in all ways, this I pray! Let's have a testimonial story and see what we can learn about witnessing anywhere. When someone is trying to run away from life, it's not easy.

To all with love,

Why a first testimony? Why build someone up? It is the desire of my heart that everyone be the best they can be. A good word is sometimes as good as a good deed. I know I have had many strange things happen in my life as called by some. To me, it's an ongoing relationship with my Lord.

We rise and fall together. When we fall, we will know the pain others feel when they fall. When we rise, we will, in turn, know the joy of the rise. Sometimes we need help to rise. I have always wanted to live in the country and thought I had the chance in 1993. It was a beautiful little twenty-acre place near Trimont, Minnesota. It, of course, needed some remodeling. No problem—I had done many remodels. After doing home remodels, you quickly notice and understand the structure of a house. In this particular house, I noticed that twelve feet of the pitched roof was blocked off and turned into a hallway. We needed to find some closet space upstairs. I thought it would be easy to open up this area with a door and finish out the spot for a closet. It would be just a small construction job, right? Wait for it! With God, all things are possible.

> He that hath an ear, let him hear what the Spirit saith unto the churches; He that over-cometh shall not be hurt of the second death. (Revelation 2:11)

I quickly opened up the area in the center of the twelve-foot area. In about one minute, I realized there had been a doorway in this center section before. There was also hardwood flooring inside the wall.

Unusual, I thought as I went to get a flashlight.

I returned to peer into the darkened opening. I saw objects in the shadows. This had already been a large storage closet at one time but had been sealed up. Why had it been sealed? I climbed through the opening I had created. I saw a large travel trunk, unlike anything I had seen before. About 1900, I guessed its age. There were two large stacks of *Life* magazines. On the top of one of the stacks was a comic book. It was dated 1939. The *Life* magazines ranged in dates from 1939 to 1942. Wait for it! I am a little slow.

I opened up the old doorway a little more and began to move the objects out to the hallway. My mind quickly reflected to asking my Father in heaven as to what this meant.

"What would you have of me, Father? A number of people have lived in this house, yet you revealed this to me."

> To give light to them that sit in darkness and *in* the shadow of death, to guide our feet into the way of peace. (Luke 1:79)

There were some old clothes—I guess boys' clothes of various seasons. I moved them out. There were some camping items: a lantern, a rolled-up mattress, and scraps on the floor. I held a flashlight on the broom handle, facing down as I swept. I thought the scraps were just something a mouse had chewed on but quickly saw a piece with some writing on it. I picked it up and stepped into the hallway to see if I could read what it was.

"Father in heaven, meet my beloved son," the writer began.

My blood froze in my veins. Tears came to my eyes. You see, I am a compassionate fellow when I sense the presence of the Holy Spirit.

The rest of the note read:

> You are my only son. (Mouse chewings.) May there one day be no more wars. You were your dad's and my life. (Mouse chewings.) May Jesus Christ help us go on with life though we may not smile again. Your last comic, that made you laugh. (Mouse chewings.)
>
> With love and tears,
> Mom and Dad

The letter was in terrible shape, but the few words left were granite. This was so painful for two people, yet my Father in heaven gave me strength at a certain season of my life. It's regrettable for a missing family connection, yet I have a heartfelt appreciation for the strangers who have been of great help in my life. We may all need a hand from someone we least expect a hand from.

The *Life* magazines were added to the collection, I guess, because of someone reading the articles about the war. This collection was a way to find peace with all that had happened. There is a God that two grieving people had to find a resolve with. There were some personal items that couldn't be thrown away but had to be concealed from sight to help find some peace. It wasn't enough to lock them into a closet, but a doorway had to be walled over to prevent entrance into the precious items. There was a lot of pain going on in this house. Only two people, I can sense, that really know the intensity of the pain going on. I have a very light grasp of the sadness, and it brings me to tears. It may sound strange to some, but I prayed for the peace of these two for a few years until I felt that they too may have passed on. Well, twenty-five years! It's now time for the gift to go forward.

Finally, *be ye* all of one mind, having compassion one of another, love as brethren, *be* pitiful, *be* courteous. (1 Peter 3:8)

Carpenters use to add small items in a void over a doorway as blessings to a home they were building. Sometimes the first owners would also add some items. This concealed room was the most heartfelt—the saddest and the bravest for me. One may think that this was not a blessing to this house, but I beg to differ. I believe it to be the greatest blessing of all.

"Father in heaven, meet my beloved son."

This letter was also a prayer with great hope and faith. "Here is my son, whom I love so dearly. Father in heaven, please take him unto your kingdom and love him as I do."

This appeared to be their only son, an only child, so one could find no comfort in holding, talking to, or saying "I love you" to another child. There was a great blame, and that happened to be World War II. My dad was in WWII and the Korean War. He never felt comfortable talking about it. Through many requests on my part, I got as much as he was willing to offer. Many think there is hope, but there are truly two pounds of pain for every pound of hope. The writer hoped for no more war.

Another great hope was to have Jesus Christ continue to help them through life. They were very defeated but knew where the only hope—the only answer—was to be found. There may not be any more smiles. One can know this, cherish Christ, and have faith but truly not be able to smile. The loss is just too great. The time would be too long. It's the "I love you" from family, friends, or perhaps even strangers. Sometimes it may be one person standing in the gap—the heartfelt prayer. Let us rise and fall together. I hold the palm of my hand open to those around me as Christ has offered his hand to me.

The comic book, which brought the last laugh to the young man, was added to the collection of concealed items. There was no

TV, limited radio, so why not the comic book? This happens to be the twenty-fifth anniversary of the procession and finding of the comic book. I had no room to keep the other items. I just don't keep things. A tool for work, but that is just about the limit. Even if one had the various items and lost them, you probably could get them replaced at some time. Take the laughter out of a home. Lock it away! The pain will grow, but they surely would have said that they had no choice. Maybe another person has to bring the smile, laughter, and the "I love you"—a new seed, if you will.

> For the wages of sin *is death*; but the gift of God *is* eternal life through Jesus Christ our Lord. (Romans 6:23)

> Verily, verily, I say unto you, He that heareth my word, and believeth on him that sent me, hath everlasting life, and shall not come into condemnation; but is passed from death unto life. (John 5:24)

It was a few weeks later when my wife and I saw the pillar of light in the grove behind the house. I don't know what this light was, or perhaps I never will. I only know it terrified my wife and she wanted to move back to town. She just said she had too much of God. This may be said by most, that this was just another house to live in. But for me, it would end up being a year of instruction from my Father in heaven. So my wife had too much God! So 99 percent of the people in the world would say the same thing. I shared this story only recently, and one person found it interesting enough to respond. I know it was strange to share an hour standing in the dark in the middle of the night talking to a pillar of light. Well, it was a pillar of light, and I have never seen one before. Thank you, Father, for letting me see this incredible event. I had a nice discussion with my Father in heaven. I was about twenty-five feet away when it disappeared. I kind of wished I hadn't gone too close. The young lady that responded was very enthused and wanted to learn more about

God and the life she could have with Jesus Christ as her savior. That is a wonderful thing! I am happy to share.

In another couple of weeks, I was hit with 220 volts of electricity or at least protected from it. You don't even come close to 220 volts and survive it. That was thoroughly informed by an electrician by the name of Jim Klima. The explosion from the ground blew an eighteen-inch-deep hole in the ground. I was pounding a steel post in the ground out in the middle of the yard. There was no indication of any electricity in the area. I lived again! Now Jim was a man of God. I had known him for a number of years and had never seen him with so much emotion. To have someone give you such a sincere hug because I had lived. How many hugs in your life do you remember?

I shall not go into a long list of other things that happened. I will reflect on why I told you this much. I wanted to go into the ministry when I got out of high school, but I turned the wrong way. When I found this hidden memory closet, I had a serious prayer about giving up everything to go into the ministry again. My life went upside down and was life-threatening over the next six months. I needed daily protection. Satan will do everything possible to destroy your life. The more you believe or the more you had believed in the past, the more he will work upon you. The earth is his. We need help!

Bad things happen to good people. That does not mean that Jesus is not with you. That does not mean he will not protect you. Learn from these times, and they will help you or prepare you for some point intended. I have a small amount of explanation for all the times I have had close calls of death, visions, words, etc. I have been told things years before they come into existence. I share them with my wife. She gives me the "oh, it's interesting." When it happens, she gives the "Oh, wow!" I say this only because we can't see the big picture or end result. It may not be the thing for us to know until the season is right—a season for all things!

To everything there is a season, and a time to every purpose under the heaven: A time to be born, and a time to die; a time to plant, and a time to pluck up that which is planted; a time to kill, and a time to heal; a time to break down, and a time to build up; a time to weep, and a time to laugh; a time to mourn, and a time to dance; a time to cast away stones, and a time to gather stones together; a time to embrace, and a time to refrain from embracing; a time to get, and a time to lose; a time to keep, and a time to cast away; a time to rend, and a time to sew; a time to keep silence, and a time to speak; a time to love, and a time to hate; a time of war, and a time of peace. What profit hath he that worketh in that wherein he laboureth? (Ecclesiastes 3:1–9)

Be the best you can be always. There are a lot of stories of hardship, joy, sadness, and of searching. To help those around you deliver the Word of God in the best light possible is so very important. I am a stranger who walks a dusty road. We all wear different shoes, but we would be hard-pressed to wear someone else shoes. I share this testimony to build you up. Always ask your Father in heaven how you can do your best for him.

Love in Christ, Fred

It's Only a Chip

February 2014

Thought: A letter for you with as much love as it can carry. May the Spirit of God direct you in all ways, this I pray! To all with love, let's have a testimonial story and see how many times we are protected from the split-second space in ongoing life.

To all with love,

The snow was very bright after an early spring snowfall. The snow was plowed well back off the edge of the highway. The roads were, of course, plowed back after the snowstorm; but for various reasons, I suppose, they were pushed back a little further off the shoulder of the road. Sometimes the snow in spring gets pushed back off the shoulder for the stability of the road. Extra water nearer the road softens the roadbed. The highway had some daytime melting and nightly dry freezing. The only ice cover was from snow packing near groves. The traffic was moving along fifty-five to sixty miles per hour. It was a beautiful bright sunny day. It was cold enough at 5:00 p.m. to prevent further thawing. Traffic was average flow for everyone seeking to go home. The vehicles were just passing each other in opposite directions at an assumed speed limit. You just respect the other drivers to stay in their lanes.

The next vehicle would just be assumed to pass like the previous one. All of a sudden, the dark-colored car went into a spin as it hit the ice patch while traveling past the grove. The car was about one hundred feet away as I started for the ditch. I was glad the shoulder had been plowed back and was frozen. I had already started slowing down, but I knew there was going to be a violent head-on collision—or did I? It was an assumption on my part.

"Sweet Jesus, have mercy?" I asked.

My heart was pounding out of my chest already. The car ahead had spun around twice already and was well into my lane. I was well over onto the shoulder, and the size of the snowbank beside me was well over four feet high.

> But be not thou far from me, O Lord: O
> my strength, haste thee to help me. (Psalm 22:19)

I was just about to turn the wheel hard into the ditch as the back end of the oncoming car was swinging toward me for the third time. I was off the road as it hit me. It took the tip of the driver's mirror off and passed on by the rest of my vehicle. I watched it pass in the mirror as I slowly brought my vehicle back onto the road and slowed down to forty miles per hour. I saw the vehicle complete the third rotation and gain control on the dry pavement. It continued on down the road as if nothing had happened. Other vehicles were coming in both directions, so I continued on my way. All of this happened in maybe ten to twelve seconds—an almost certain head-on collision to it's just another sunny day.

Why had this happened? I would think that almost everyone that can drive would ask this question. It would probably be followed up with "Boy, was I lucky." How many times does one think that another vehicle could easily cross the center line of the highway and you would find someone in your lane of travel? If and when this would happen, how many times would you come out untouched? Would you be ready to give God any credit for his protection?

I give God a thank-you for being alive every day. I ask God every day for protection against what I can see and that which I cannot see.

> For he shall give his angels charge over thee,
> to keep thee in all thy ways. (Psalm 91:11)

I immediately thanked my sweet Lord and savior, Jesus Christ, for his protection. I couldn't live without knowing he has sent the Holy Spirit or his legion of angels to watch over me. It really makes you feel loved. I thank God that everything is not so dynamic. I know it is just a little different for each person to believe in God and to find their way to Jesus Christ. The Bible tells of the hardening of the heart and the searing of the conscience. It is possible to develop yourself in a way, which pushes you away from believing in Jesus. One must make a little effort. It is as simple as a yes or no each day. If we say yes or no to speeding in a car, we can say yes or no to salvation. The rewards are unbelievable in both cases.

The feeling of not wanting to accept time with God is human nature. It is something referred to as sin. It is sin that keeps us separated from God and our creator. I have had many tell me they just don't have time for God.

"Do you have time for breathing?" I have sometimes responded. If you can take a handful of dirt and create a human being, you probably don't need God.

> For God so loved the world, that he gave his only begotten Son, that whosoever believeth in him should not perish, but have everlasting life. For God sent not his Son into the world to condemn the world; but that the world through him might be saved. He that believeth on him is not condemned: but he that believeth not is condemned already, because he hath not believed in the name of the only begotten Son of God. (John 3:16–18)

Love in Christ, Fred

Candles, Rocks, and Love

March 2014

Thought: A letter for you with as much love as it can carry. May the Spirit of God direct you in all ways, this I pray! To all with love, let's have a testimonial story and see what we can learn about the oldest man I ever met. Go meet a stranger! This is secondhand, but I believe it to be true.

To all with love,

I didn't think this would be a story that I would write, but the Holy Spirit compels me to do so. A preacher by the name of Matt Leroy gave a very good sermon that I wish all could have heard. I had never met this young man, but my soul leaped for joy the moment I saw him. I wish he was my next-door neighbor. I love that man.

John Andersen was ninety-four years old when I first met him. He had farmed with his wife, Mary, all of their lives and then retired to a small home in town. I was doing a project in this town, and each day for a couple of days, I drove by this small house on my way home. On the third day, I waved to him as I drove by. He responded with a half-lifted arm. The fourth day I saw him, I stopped and visited for a bit.

John was a tall thin man and spoke very clearly. He spoke in detail as if to savor the conversation. The conversation was slow and well thought out. He had been married to Mary for seventy years and now had missed her for a half dozen years. There were no children living, and there was no other family around for some years. He claimed to be tired and felt he was just withering away. He said he felt important that I would take the time to stop and visit.

I love to hear stories of life, so it didn't take me long to ask John if he could reflect such things to me. To my surprise, John was excited that I cared about his life. He and Mary had always wanted a child to share such things with.

"You don't know the longing and sadness of wanting a family unless you had experienced such an emotion," John reflected to me. John reflected several things to me, but this particular story needs to be shared.

The weather had been warm all week with the hint of spring peeking through the frozen landscape. It had been some time since they had been to town, and supplies were in great need. Money was in need to get these things, so they would load the wagon with sacks of grain to trade at the local supply store. It was a very long day to town and back, so Mary would stay home and care for the livestock. It was the usual manner to give each other a hug and a kiss goodbye.

Mary was a bit shorter than John, so the hug may sweep her off her feet. John often remarked that he would sweep Mary off her feet every day of her life. It was their private joke of endearment, and John cracked a smile as he reflected a thought of days gone by. John turned the team of horses around to head down the lane as he gave a wave to Mary. She stood on the porch of their little three-room home. It was a familiar sight which John often reflected back to over the years.

Even though it was quite nice out, Mary had insisted that John would take a heavy coat with him. It was called a buffalo coat. John chuckled to himself as he sat on the coat. He didn't think he needed it, but it was great to sit on. It was a great cushion for his backside. Mary had also insisted on warming rocks and wrapping them in a burlap sack for his feet. He pushed the rocks around under his feet as he drove the team. They were quite useful for keeping your feet warm. He didn't think he needed these either, but Mary had gone to a lot of attention in preparing these rocks and putting them in the seat box of the wagon. She had also prepared a sack with sandwiches, a jar of canned apples, and a jar of milk. Mary was a thoughtful person and gave it all to him. There was no one but him to hear and the horses as he whispered, "I love you, Mary." He had done that often, so this time was not unusual. John spoke to Mary even when she was not there with him.

You rarely saw anyone going to town or returning. When you got close to town, you would see other folks. It was a ride of solitude. When John cleared the wooded area of their farm, the land opened up. There was only an occasional clump of trees here and there for most of the way, so the ride became fairly uneventful. John had only been on his way for about two hours when a few light flakes of snow began to fall. He thought he may be close to halfway to his destination. A few flakes of snow were no alarm to him. This had happened many times in his thirty-seven years of life.

In just a few minutes, the snow began to fall at a steady rate. John flicked the reins a couple of times, as he recalled, quickening the pace of the team. He didn't want to go too fast as it was a long haul. The load was as big as it could possibly have been loaded.

It wasn't but another ten minutes when the wind started to blow. There weren't a lot of good landmarks, so it would be easy to end up going in circles. John pulled his buffalo coat on as he drove the team.

"Thank you, Mary," he whispered.

It wouldn't matter if you were one mile or ten miles from town. Lost would be lost just the same. John saw a small clump of about twenty trees he recognized, so he pulled the team in on the side, which gave him the most protection from the wind. He would just have to wait for the snow to let up. After twenty minutes or so, he got down from the wagon and tied the horses to a tree. He walked around the clump of trees. There were a lot of dead branches and tall grass. He backed the team up and led them a little further into the trees so they could eat the tall grass. He watched the horses move the snow around with their muzzles to get at the grasses.

The wind began to whip the snow into his face. *How to get out of the wind?* he thought. He had a wagon with sacks of grain and a tarp over the grain. He began to loosen the tarp on one side and climbed up on the load. Placing the sacks in a fortified fashion, he hollowed out an area in the middle of the wagon. He left the bottom layer of sacks in place to give him some comfort off the bottom of the wagon. The tarp was tightened down, with a small opening in the back of the wagon. He came out of his makeshift shelter only to be gifted with a face full of snow. The snow was relentless. It was a storm, and it meant business, he contemplated.

John went up to the wagon box and retrieved the bag of rocks, the food bag, a jar of milk, and his rifle. He pushed his items into the opening of his shelter, quickly following the items in and securing the opening. It was quite dark inside the shelter. The rock bag still had a little heat in it, so he placed it by his feet. His hands were a little cold, so he opened the rock bag to let his hands have a little of the heat.

"Thank you, Mary," he whispered.

With warm hands, he opened the sack, which contained his lunch. It was too dark to see, so he was lost. John felt around in the sack, and his hand came into contact with what felt like a candle—a thick sturdy candle—then a second and a third candle.

John laughed and whispered, "What am I to do with these?" He had no matches on him. He felt around in the sack, and his hand soon detected a small bundle of matches tied up tight with a piece of string. He struck a match and lit a candle. He carefully put the candle in between two sacks of grain. The candle illuminated the small area and began to give off some heat.

"Thank you, Mary," he whispered. He gave a little laugh as he thought of his Mary thinking of everything.

John retrieved his sandwiches and began to remove the wrapping of brown paper. To his surprise, he found a note tucked under the string around the sandwiches. A smile came to his face as he felt like a newlywed after fifteen years of marriage. He carefully opened the note and held it near the candle to reveal its secret.

My dearest John,

May my hands be gifted from God to help you in time of need? May my father in heaven teach me the wisdom to foresee all ways to help you? May my love for you be with you both near and far? May you feel the love from my Father in heaven, as I do? May his Spirit comfort you and his Son give you salvation.

This is my prayer and love,
Mary

John read the note over and over as he ate his lunch. Mary read the Bible every evening and sometimes read it to him whether he wanted to hear it or not. Her laugh and smile pulled him into the words. He couldn't help but be drawn into the message the way she presented it. There wasn't a church close, so Mary insisted she would be their church. God didn't need a building! Mary always wanted John to believe as she did.

The cold began to penetrate his surroundings, so John lit the other two candles. The heat revealed itself immediately. The tarp began to sag, so John hit it up with his hand a few times to release it of its load of snow. He quickly opened a few sacks of grain so he could get some around himself to help insulate his body. He soon found himself comfortable and went back to his prized possession, the note. John studied the note intently with only an occasional blast of wind across the tarp to distract him. It was like he was detained with one mission and one only—to observe the message in this note. Mary had often said that the most important part of life was to find the way to live now and later. Salvation through Jesus Christ is what she would say. He would just agree even if he couldn't quite believe in what she said. She was a bundle of love, a magnet of happiness. Her anger was nothing more than a mild frustration.

John reached for the sack of rocks. He put his hand in the sack but felt no heat. He pulled one out and saw the little knitted cover, which the rock was in. It looked blue. He pulled another one out and observed it had a green cover. Still, he pulled another, and it was red. He held the three rocks, each which was the size of the palm of your hand. He felt a tear come to his eye.

"I love you, Mary," he whispered. "Thank you, Son of God! Thank you for sending me Mary. I don't know you, but if you are anything like the Mary you sent me, I am all for you."

At that moment, in that situation, John felt like a light had just been turned on. All the things Mary had told him, read to him, and enlightened him with rushed into his soul.

"You have created me, Father. I have sinned and brought grief to you. Father, you have sent your son, Jesus Christ, to give me salvation. I repent of my sins. You have blessed me with my Mary. Now she has revealed you to me through her love for me. Your love is now greater than I can comprehend. Thank you, Mary! Thank you, Jesus Christ, son of my Mary's God," John whispered into the night, into the storm, and under the canvas.

"I believe," John whispered. "Was this moment created for me just to help me believe? It's strange. I don't remember crying in my life, but I cried so it made me feel weak on my knees. I cried for my sinful self, I cried for my sins to be forgiven, I cried for the love Mary gave me, and I cried for the situation my Father created to help me believe. I shall not waste another day not believing."

And it repented the LORD that he had made man on the earth, and it grieved him at his heart. (Genesis 6:6)

For all have sinned, and come short of the glory of God. (Romans 3:23)

For God so loved the world, that he gave his only begotten Son, that whosoever believeth in him should not perish, but have everlasting life. For God sent not his Son into the world to condemn the world; but that the world through him might be saved. (John 3:16–17)

Love in Christ, Fred

In a Second

April 2014

Thought: A letter for you with as much love as it can carry. May the Spirit of God direct you in all ways, this I pray! Let's have a testimonial story and see what we can learn about our Father's protection when life threatens.

To all with love,

The first-testimony story for June changed this week as a split second of life flashing before my eyes has compelled me to do so. How many times has a second been good for me? May the Holy Spirit move, guide, and comfort each one that reads this testimony! May this be a blessing unto you! Many things can happen to us in a single second. I am a creation that breathes and eats food. Only my Father in heaven can create all three of these, so only my Father deserves worship and credit for all.

It was a few days before Christmas, and we were offered a wonderful invitation to visit some relatives in Round Lake, Minnesota. It was a cold day, but sunshine leads you toward disbelief of what the temperature indicated. Upon arriving at our destination, we were impressed with the twelve inches of new snow. The farmyard had its huge piles of mounded-up snow. Little dozy children soon become awakened at the thrill of some snow activities. Once bundled up in snow suits, coats, boots, hats, scarves, and mittens, they had grown to be twice their size. They were, however, ready for anything to do outside.

Our host was busily working on his snowmobile. It was a tool for him to use around the farm, but he thought we may have a bit of fun riding it around the farm and the lake he lived on. We had never driven or had ridden on a snowmobile, so it sounded exciting to have the opportunity. He gave rides to each of us and then instructed me on its operation. I soon had the instructions down and took over giving the kids rides. I was informed on how to go down onto the lake and I could ride from one end to the other without any concerns. The kids were only five and seven, so I would give them a ride in front of me to be able to hold onto them as well.

When they got tired of riding and wanted to go into the house, I shuffled them up to the house. I figured this may be a one-time opportunity. I decide to drive the snowmobile for a bit longer. I started driving a bit farther down the lake. Out on the lake, the wind shifted the snow around a bit more. Visibility became limited from time to time. Most of the time, I spent riding along the shoreline and investigating what was to be seen. I soon could see the end of the lake, which I was informed of. I had seen the shoreline, and it had curved a fair distance into an arc, so I decided to cut back at a straight line toward the farmhouse. With the new twelve-inch snowfall, the wind had plenty to play with. The line of sight went up and down from zero visibility to maybe up to seventy feet.

I began the ride back, but the blustering snow was blowing toward me, again reducing my visibility. I thought I would speed up and hurry back. After all, there was nothing to be seen out here away from the shore, right? I was about a third of the way back and moving along at a very fast pace. I suddenly saw open water and just couldn't believe it. My blood froze. There were about forty feet of open water. All I could think of was to lean and steer to the left toward the shoreline. I was at least two hundred yards from shore. I was only about thirty feet from the water when I first saw it. I definitely saw myself going into the water.

"Jesus, forgive me of my sins and have mercy on my soul," I whispered. I had just prepared to hit the cold water and saw no other means. It was near zero degrees, so there was no surviving the cold water. I felt an unknown urge to accelerate as I leaned to the left, away from the water source. This was all happening within seconds. Water began to spray the air as the track of the snowmobile stopped finding all snow. All along the right side, I saw water, but there was snow to the left. At a distance, I thought I had seen about forty feet of water, but now it was much more as I went speeding by. The spray of water was now more than a mist; it was shower time.

Just when it seemed as if an unavoidable peril was about to happen, the track stopped throwing up water and found snow. I found a comfort point and slowed down to take a look back at the water. The blowing snow was now at my back, and I could see more clearly. How did I ever get around or over the water was a miracle to me?

I stopped the snowmobile and reflected on my savior Jesus Christ. I felt spent as the rush of adrenaline had used me up upon what I had just viewed as an impending death. Yet one more time in my life, I live. My only question is why? "Do you yet have a purpose for me, Father?"

I had survived the veil of death many times in my life. This was just one more time, but I had as much gratitude as I ever had. I shed a tear or two of gratitud, to say the least. A second or two is all I had, but our Father in heaven has limitless time. Father, you see all, and you would catch me and save me from my own peril? I say be strong in the Lord Jesus Christ, and he will be strong for you when peril is at hand. I sat looking at the water and watching the wind ripple at its surface.

> "I am Alpha and Omega, the beginning and the ending," saith the Lord, which is, and which was, and which is to come, the Almighty. (Revelation 1:8)

I gave my Father all the praise I could deliver the rest of the way back to the farm. I parked the snowmobile as I just couldn't find the interest to ride it anymore. I had a discussion with my host as to his knowledge of the open water area. He knew there was a spring at that end of the lake, but he never knew it didn't freeze over. He had lived there for over forty years and found it hard to believe. I reflected on the thought of impending death and how quickly life can see an end.

When I offered this reflection, he related to the years he was in World War II. As an excellent marksman, he was assigned duties to often scout out advances of troops. It seemed to be a difficult thing to talk about for him, so I didn't press for details. I knew he was a man of very strong character in many ways, yet he felt life was at its last many times. You don't really know what one goes through in combat situations unless you have been there. I have not and thank my Father in heaven for not having a war when I graduated. My dad saw a lot of bad things in WWII and in the Korean War. He asked me to not go into the service unless I was requested to do so. To sit for days at a time and shoot the so-called enemy from great distances has one mindset, but to shoot someone face to face is quite another. You go from feeling like a human being with a job to do to an animal fighting for life.

> Let us therefore come boldly unto the throne of grace, that we may obtain mercy, and find grace to help in time of need. (Hebrews 4:16)

My host reflected on God and having mercy on his soul for what he had to do while my dad couldn't believe that God had created such a world to live in. My dad had a lot of close-quarter fighting as well as being in Japan two weeks after the dropping of the atomic bombs. I would never want to wear my dad's shoes. I would also never want to wear my host's shoes. I have prayed many times for my Father to have mercy on both of these men. I have a great hope for one yet a great sadness for the other.

> Not by works of righteousness which we have done, but according to his mercy he saved us, by the washing of regeneration, and renewing of the Holy Ghost. (Titus 3:5)

Many times we come so close to having the fragile source of life being taken away. I was on the highway leaving Sioux Falls with my wife when we were approaching a crossroad known as Ellis Road. The light had turned red, so we came to a stop. A fuel transport semi was about 150 yards from the intersection and moving about fifty miles per hour. As I waited there, I reflected out loud that the truck is not going to stop. In fact, it never even slowed down. The cross light turned green, and a young lady with her kids in a van started to move toward the intersection. I found my teeth starting to clench. The truck flew through the intersection and never slowed. If the van had started to move just a little quicker, one second, everyone near the intersection wouldn't be here today. It would have been an explosion. I think the young lady didn't see the truck because it was moving so fast. The truck driver never saw the intersection for some reason. The van crossed right behind the truck with a paused stop, I guess from shock. Split seconds! If the truck hit the van, it would have hit us head-on. Shall I say split tenths of a second! Be prepared as the kingdom of God may be upon you in split tenths of a second!

Love in Christ, Fred

I Am Too Hurt to Believe

May 2014

Thought: A letter for you with as much love as it can carry. May the Spirit of God direct you in all ways, this I pray! Let's have a testimonial story and see what we can learn about witnessing anywhere. When someone is trying to run away from life, it's not easy.

To all with love,

It was after eleven on a Saturday night. I had wanted to finish plumbing a project house. I avoided working on Sunday to do what I could to honor God. I have had many jobs in which working on Sunday was required. To not have to work on Sunday is a blessing. I quickly threw my tools in the truck and hurried to get home. I lived just fifteen miles away in another town. A predestined time was set for being home. There were no cell phones or any phones as far as that goes. I was headed for Interstate 90, but suddenly I found myself going down old Highway 16. I usually went down Interstate 90. I felt compelled to go down Highway 16. I don't really know how I got on old Highway 16, but once I was on it, I just said, "Oh well," and continued on toward Sherburn, Minnesota. Why am I going on 16? It takes longer!

I was about a third of the way home when I saw a green Station Wagon parked on the side of the highway, with no lights on. I just figured someone had left the vehicle as I just passed around it. When I passed the car, I thought I saw someone sitting in the driver's seat. The road was quiet, and there may not be any other traffic for some time. I was compelled to turn around and go back to investigate with another quick look. It was late, and I needed to get home. Maybe someone just wanted to sit alongside the road. I pulled a U-turn in the highway and drove back past the Station Wagon and observed the driver's seat as I passed. There was someone definitely in that position. I pulled another U-turn past the car and pulled in behind the wagon. I had no idea what to expect. I simply placed myself into God's hands as I got out of my pickup. I was told constantly to not stop and pick up strangers.

It was very dark, I thought, as I looked for some stars or moonlight. It was cloudy, and no light was to be had except for the lights from my pickup, which I left on with the truck running. The sweet smell of corn pollinating was filling the air. It reminded me of watermelon for some reason. It was very quiet, with only an occasional cricket chirping. There was hardly a hint of a breeze as I walked up to the side of the green Station Wagon. As I stood at the driver's door, I saw a woman in about her midtwenties. She had some tissues and appeared to have been crying.

"Do you believe in God?" the woman asked through the closed window. The question felt shocking.

"Very much so," I replied.

The window began to crank down with a squeak at every turn.

"I am sorry, but I am afraid. My name is Julie," she added.

"My name is Fred," I responded. "What's the problem here?"

"I have a flat tire, and there is no spare tire," Julie informed me.

"I could give you a ride home," I suggested.

I noticed a small boy sleeping in the backseat. "You have a child in the back with you?"

"Yes," she informed me.

The crying made me a little uncomfortable, yet I felt sorry for her. The situation felt very personal.

While letting Julie cry, I prayed for God to send his Holy Spirit for guidance. A sudden gust of wind blew and rustled the corn all of a sudden. It was more than a small gust; it was a blast. It made the hair on my neck rise. My knees went weak as if God was going to appear. It gave me a chill. It was a huge blast, which left as suddenly as it came. I looked around and only saw blackness. It startled me. It's like asking for something, and it arrives before you ask.

"What? What? Father, may your hand do as it wills," I whispered.

"What does that mean?" Julie asked.

"Oh, I spoke a thought out loud and didn't think you heard me," I responded. "I talk out loud or whisper thoughts to God all the time. Every breath I take is a breath I get from my Father in heaven."

"Do you really believe in God so much that you speak words to him just like now in front of a stranger?" Julie asked.

"I actually am thinking about laying my hands on your car and asking my Father to repair your tire," I responded. "I don't feel compelled to do so, so I won't."

I have actually laid my hand on a car and asked God to make it move. Before I did this, I informed the driver that I was going to do this and it was for the benefit of the driver, which God was waiting for them to believe. The car would not work, and the driver had called a tow truck. They had tried everything normal.

When I said, "God will make your car work" and I told her to put it into drive and then reverse and it worked, she was speechless. At that point, the tow truck pulled up and had to be dismissed. The car is still moving almost a year later without any mechanical work. Every time I see this person, I ask if they are praying. God is waiting. This just happened last year, but back to our testimony. With God, all things are possible—all things!

"Julie?" I started. You asked me if I believed in God, do you?"

"I don't think I do anymore," Julie said slowly. Life, marriage, and work just seem like a mess," she replied through the sniffles.

"Okay, I believe enough for both of us," I replied with a smile. "So you believed at one time. Everyone has ups and downs throughout life. It does seem a little unfair. If your tire was not flat, where were you going?" I asked.

"To my parents in Iowa. It's a couple of hundred miles," Julie detailed.

"Do you live around here?" I asked.

"No," Julie stated.

"I believe you had a flat for a reason," I began. "It feels like you are trying to run away from something. I will not go into details, but I tried to run away twice in my life, and God put a detour in my path both times. If he hadn't, I may not be here today. I will take you home if you like," I offered.

"It's too far for you to do that," Julie spoke in a surprised voice.

"The distance doesn't matter," I offered. "Ask of me what you will," I added. "You may or may not believe that the Holy Spirit gave you a flat tire or God sent me to talk to you because for some reason, I ended up going down Highway 16 when I usually take the interstate."

"Can you take me into town to see if I can get a tire for my car?" Julie asked.

"I certainly can, but the only station open is the Road Runner on the interstate," I sympathetically offered.

Julie quietly asked, "Let's try there, okay?"

"Yes, we will go," I encouraged.

We got in the truck with a very sleepy Tommy sitting between us. I explained the work I was doing on the small house and how I repaired them as a part-time job. It was unusually late for me to be working and not yet home, I explained. Julie asked where the small house was and how much it would be worth. It will have a value of about 55K when finished. I explained how I got repo homes from a local bank. The bank would just call me and ask if I wanted another home. I could do this for a full-time job, but I choose to do it only part-time. I didn't think anything of it at the time. I just thought Julie was curious. It was just searching for small talk, I was thinking.

"Here is the station," I announced the obvious as we pulled in and parked. "Do you have any road service on your car insurance?" I asked.

"No, we don't have insurance," Julie explained.

We got out of the truck and walked inside the convenience store to talk to the clerk. He assured us that the downtown station would help us at 7:00 a.m. but not until then.

"I will just stay here at the store until then," Julie suggested.

"No, we need to do something more," I suggested.

"I don't have enough money for a tire and a hotel," Julie responded with a defeated voice. I could see she was trying not to cry, but there were silent tears running down her face. Tommy was hanging onto her waist, trying to sleep.

"Julie, ask of me what you will?" I offered.

"You say things strangely," Julie responded.

"Well, there is no value in anything, but in the hand of God your Father, you shall have untold treasure," I offered.

I was never to bring someone to our home especially at midnight. My wife would never allow that.

"Dear Jesus, all I have is yours. Show me the way. Show me the way."

I stood staring out the window when I saw a sign across the street with a $19.00 per night fee. I looked in my billfold; I had $27.00. I quickly took the dollars out of my billfold and returned it to my pocket.

"Let's take you to the hotel across the street and get you a room. Here are some dollars for you," as I held out the money.

"Why?" Julie asked.

"It's the right thing to do," I answered. "I want you to think back on this moment and know that Jesus Christ loves you. He came into this world to give his life for you, me, and all that will accept him. Is there anything else I can do for you?" I asked.

"No, we are good," Julie offered encouragingly. "You have been very helpful. You help me believe. My Father in heaven owns houses on a thousand hills. May he bless yours!"

"Thank you, but I just want you to be okay," I offered appreciatively.

"I will never forget," Julie whispered. Julie held her hand up, and I thought she was waving goodbye. I held my hand up in return as I turned to leave when I realized she was pointing toward heaven.

When I left the two strangers, I was perplexed. To make a statement that my Father owns houses on a thousand hills didn't really seem like something that one who was down spiritually would say. Was this all she needed to feel strengthened? The rush of wind in the cornfield was something I will never forget. Some may just call it a sudden gust of wind while I call it the breath of God, the Holy Spirit, for all things ended well.

> And Elijah said, "*As* the LORD of hosts liveth, before whom I stand, I will surely shew myself unto him to day." (1 Kings 18:15)

> But these are written, that ye might believe that Jesus is the Christ, the Son of God; and that believing ye might have life through his name. (John 20:31)

> Whom having not seen, ye love; in whom, though now ye see *him* not, yet believing, ye rejoice with joy unspeakable and full of glory. (1 Peter 1:8)

> Now the God of hope fill you with all joy and peace in believing, that ye may abound in hope, through the power of the Holy Ghost. (Romans 15:13)

Three days later, I received a phone call. I was offered $5,000 over my current costs of what I had put into my little renovation house. I was to figure up all I had done and any costs I had incurred in the purchase of the property. I could have a check for that amount as soon as the paperwork was finished. I did, and I had a check within the month. I was very surprised about all that had happened. In my mind, I refer to this event as the conversation in the cornfield. I have sold a lot of homes, but this sale was the most unusual. Was it a blessing from the act I had done? Perhaps, but then I consider every breath a blessing.

Julie was a scared person and not sure if she still believed in our Father Supreme and savior Jesus Christ. When we departed, she was stating that her heavenly Father owns houses on a thousand hills. She was lifting her arm, I believe, toward heaven and not waving to me as I had first thought. The next thing I know is I have a huge blessing. Be aware! Lend a hand in some way to a friend, neighbor, or a stranger. An appreciation of a lending hand could be an answer to their prayer. It could be blessings on you! I don't look for blessings from my Father when I do something for someone, but it does bring a tear or two when something comes my way. It is just him saying, "I love you. I really do."

I have enclosed another testimony from such a person. May the Holy Spirit comfort and care for these lovely people always.

> Nevertheless I tell you the truth; it is expedient for you that I go away: for if I go not away, the Comforter will not come unto you; but if I depart, I will send him unto you. (John16:7)

> But the Comforter, *which is* the Holy Ghost, whom the Father will send in my name, he shall teach you all things, and bring all things to your remembrance, whatsoever I have said unto you. (John14:26)

Love in Christ, Fred

Lost in Old Beliefs

June 2014

Thought: A letter for you with as much love as it can carry. May the Spirit of God direct you in all ways, this I pray! Let's look into a testimonial story to show you how paths of each other can cross for a short time and last forever. Also remember that the color of your soul is not what you see!

To all with love,

At this time in my life, I was renting a couple of homes out as extra income. I did this in addition to my full-time job at a local hardware store in Jackson, Minnesota.

A local banker had approached me in the store one day and said, "Oh, I hear you are a hard worker."

"Thank you for the compliment, and yes, it is necessary to provide for my family," I replied.

"Would you like to take a quick look at a house after work?"

"It can't hurt. I will see you at the home after work."

A mysterious door had just been opened. What hand can open and close any doors? It was one of those head-scratching moments.

I looked at the first home, and it needed a lot of work. The banker said he would finance the home with no down payment or loan costs if I would fix it up.

"I will pray about it and get back to you tomorrow," I responded.

"Pray about it?" the banker asked with a bit of a frown.

"Sure," I replied with a smile as I reached forward to shake his hand.

To the banker, I became known as his friend in Christ! Sweet! He also helped me, but the rest of the homes was at as low of price as possible. See God's hand yet?

> I know thy works: I have set before thee an
> open door, and no man can shut it: for thou hast
> a little strength, and has kept my word, and hast
> not denied my name. (Revelation 3:8)

We serve a God of open doors. When he opens a door, no devil can shut it; and when he closes a door, no devil can open it. That is the God we serve!

The number of homes grew to eighteen in a short time. It would take about four or five thousand dollars and a lot of labor to get them ready to live in. In this town, no one wanted to rent to Laotian people. The love in my heart would not allow me to be a copy of what was around me. Now there is prejudice and ridicule to last a lifetime in this small town. Most of the Laotian people were helpers to the United States during the Vietnam War. They wanted to live like they were used to in a third-world country. I will not mention all the hatred I received, but to get the picture, I was spit on walking down the street many times. I taught many of them how to live the United States way just to help them fit in! This was living by the hand of God in many ways.

When I went to sleep that night, I prayed instead of sleeping. After many hours of wrestling with God and much discussion, I would accept what the banker had to offer. As the months went by, I ended up with eighteen homes. May God receive the glory! It helped provide a good life for several years. The work was hard but still gratifying.

In the rental of these homes, I held no prejudice for anyone. There were very few that would rent to Laotians. It was for many reasons I am sure, like the third-world style of living, beliefs, and communication. I have always believed in doing the best I could do. It's like this work is for the Lord Jesus Christ.

On a particular Saturday, I received a phone call from a particular Laotian family. We shall call them Jon and Kim. Jon and Kim had one child, which was absolutely everything to them. We will call him Brent. The little two-bedroom home they rented from me made them very happy. Whenever they saw me, they would always express great gratitude and appreciation. The home had its colorful mats and pillows in the living room. The bedrooms had their rolled-up mats and small wooden dressers with their clothing. The mats were by the door, where the shoes would come off and the slippers would be put on. It appears to be all good, but is it?

They were pleasant, hardworking folks. They had asked if I could be there at one to look at a drain that they couldn't get to work. I would be there.

When I arrived, Jon was at the door and was happy to see me.

"Please, please come in." The door opened into the small porch and that led into the kitchen.

"Is it the kitchen sink that is clogged?" I asked.

"Please, please come into the living room," Jon beckoned.

I followed him into the next room and found Kim and Brent standing there, smiling and happy to see me. However, sitting on the floor were two young ladies with thin sheets wrapped around their bodies but shoulders exposed. I quickly turned around and left the home. I went out and sat on the front steps.

> Flee immorality. Every other sin that a man commits is outside the body, but the immoral man sins against his own body. Or do you not know that your body is a temple of the Holy Spirit who is in you, whom you have from God, and that you are not your own? (1 Corinthians 6:18–19)

Jon came out with a frown and asked, "What is the problem?"

"I don't approve, Jon. You know I have a family. There is to be one man, one woman, and to be married. This is consecrated by the one and only God. Do you not believe this to be so?"

"Yes, but they have no husbands and are alone," Jon replied.

"Jon, Jon," I whispered as I pat him on the shoulder, "Jesus Christ is my Lord and Savior. Jesus Christ is everything to me. He forgives me when I do wrong, but I would not want to do anything to provoke him to anger. Would you ever have more than one wife?"

Jon responded that he would consider it if he could afford it.

"Do you even have a clogged sink?" I asked.

"No," Jon offered reluctantly.

"Jon," you have hurt me. You lied to get me here. You offered me a young lady with no right. In this country, you can only have one wife. It's the law! Even if you don't believe in the God I do, you have to follow the laws of this country. Many people don't, and there are consequences for not following the laws, whether it is more than one wife or speeding with a car. I know, Jon, how much you love Brent. Jesus loves us all many times more than that. Jon, I forgive you, and you will not even understand what I am saying. Jon, my God would tell me to run from this situation. I wish you could believe, Jon."

God did forgive everybody, but he doesn't force us to accept his forgiveness. It's a free gift, but the recipient of a gift still has to accept that gift. We are only forgiven if we accept God's forgiveness through Jesus Christ (*Superbook*).

I left and I only wished I had more words for Jon and his family. In the next week, Jon and Kim bought a Z28 for Brent. It was a graduation present. Brent took it out that weekend for a drive. He obviously wanted to see how fast it would go. It was estimated he was doing 160 mph when he crashed and killed himself instantly.

In the middle of the week, Jon called and asked if I could stop after work and unclog the kitchen drain. I said I would stop, but in my mind, I thought it had something to do with Brent just getting killed. Did having a clogged drain mean something more than what I thought it was?

When I arrived, I knocked on the door but noticed there were several wraps of cord string running around the outside of the house.

Jon came walking up to me from the garage.

"Jon, I am so sorry for your loss. I know Brent was Kim's and your life."

"My life will have no more happiness," Jon replied while he just stared at the ground.

"What is this cord string running around the house?" I asked.

"It is seven strands to keep out the evil spirits," Jon said.

"Cord string is only string. Put your belief into a source that gives life, growth, and love. Have these strings done anything for you? If not, I will help you remove them," I suggested.

So Jon took out a knife and began to cut the strings. I helped him remove them. "Jon, do we still have a clogged drain?"

"The kitchen drain is still clogged," Jon replied.

We went into the house, and I turned on the water in the sink. The water didn't go down. "I need to go down the basement and see if there is a clean out for the drain, Jon."

I went down the stairs to the basement, and Jon followed me. I flipped the light on at the bottom of the stairs, and something went running across the floor. "What was that?" I asked Jon.

"It's a spotted chicken," Jon responded.

"Why is there a chicken down here?" I asked.

"It is to keep evil spirits out of the house," Jon informed me.

"Jon, Jon, my good friend Jon, would you rather have me for a friend or a chicken in your basement?" I asked Jon as I looked at him eye to eye. "Do you really believe a chicken is going to keep out a spirit?"

"No, I don't know. I guess not." Jon fished for an answer with his responses.

"Take the chicken out! Are you doing anything else in the house," I asked firmly.

"No, nothing else," Jon said in a whisper.

"By the hand of my God, I will have no part of these beliefs. This home shall be a loving home to all who enter in," I commanded in a loud voice, which made Jon take a step back. "I see no clean out for the sink. Let's go back upstairs and look at the trap under the sink," I instructed.

We went back upstairs to the kitchen sink. I noticed there was no water in the sink, which I had run earlier. I turned the water on and let it run. It continued to run freely, with no signs of a clog.

"There was a clog, really there was," Jon spurted out in disbelief. "I saw the water in the sink before, but it's all good now."

"Believe, Jon, just believe," I offered as I just stood looking into Jon's face.

"I have to go," Jon whispered as if he had seen something he couldn't explain.

God is calling his people to face evil in this world with the truth of Scripture and with boldness. When God made a covenant with Israel on Mount Sinai, he told them to have no false gods. In the days of Elijah, the children of Israel went after the false gods. Their sin led to prophet Elijah challenging the false prophets (1 Kings 18:15).

The same thing happens in our lives, families, churches, and communities. When we make a commitment to live for God, we will face conflict with evil. Just like Elijah, God will give each of us power and wisdom through the Holy Spirit to confront whatever evil may stand in opposition to the plan of God.

Love in Christ, Fred

Sweep Me Away

Thought: A letter for you with as much love as it can carry. May the Spirit of God direct you in all ways, this I pray! Let's have a testimonial story and see what we can learn about protection from the unseen.

To all with love,

Some stories are difficult to explain, but I do so to the best of my ability. My only purpose is to give God the glory he deserves. My next hope would be that those who read these stories would find as much purpose as I have found. There may be more details than one cares to read, but I am compelled to write this way. I pray over these stories and ask for guidance. I give this freely as it was given to me freely.

We had just moved back into our small home in Sherburn, Minnesota, a couple of weeks ago. There had been a fire a few days before Christmas. The fire had forced us to move into an apartment. For a family of five, it was a little small. We knew it would only be for about six months. We couldn't do all the work as I was busy working at the local co-op. The insurance didn't cover very much of the loss, so we had to do as much of the work as we could ourselves. The original part of the home was the first Assembly of God church in the town. A good portion of that structure was still intact. The floor and part of the walls were okay in the other half. It had an old rock foundation, but it was decided by the bank mostly to keep everything we could and rebuild.

The most amazing part about this rebuild was that only one person from a block and a half down the street came by to offer a casserole for our supper when I was working on the house one evening. We were left with only the clothes on our backs. Nothing from the church we went to, the church we visited with friends on Sunday evenings, the gas customers that I offered twenty-four-hour service to for the last three years, and nothing from friends that I had known for years. I could have asked my brothers or parents for help, but I didn't. I give everything I can but never ask for anything in return. When it comes right down to it, are people really so self-centered? I found this astounding.

There is a season and a reason for everything under heaven. The little home was back on track, and we liked it. I would have to find part-time work. Most families do when they have children anyway. I was happy that I had walked downstairs when I did. I had only gone to bed about an hour and a half ago. The girls had gone down at eight. I was a poor sleeper and had a habit of getting up for every little thing. As I walked to the sink, I thought I saw the edge of the kitchen ceiling on fire. We had just had a local handyman install a small wood-burning stove. I walked out into the porch and saw the ceiling on fire. I quickly got dressed and grabbed one bundled-up sleepy kid after another and brought them out to the car in the driveway. I knew the fire was beyond my control when I first saw it. The next thing I did was call the fire department. Then I took the kids to Grandma's. My ex-wife, Carol, had a part-time job at a small restaurant in town, so I let her know what was going on. So the fire took the house, but I was ever so thankful for God's mercy in protecting us.

So after moving back into our home, the first thing we did was to thank God and ask him for his continued protection from that which we can see and that which we cannot see. The home seemed complete. The kids were happy with their room even if it was just one room to share. Our bedroom was right across from theirs by means of a small four-foot landing at the top of the stairs. We always left the hall landing light on so if the kids got up, they could see and not fall down the stairs. We also left our door and their door open so we could see their room.

It was after 1:00 a.m., and we had been sleeping for about two hours. Suddenly Carol screamed and then said, "What's that?"

I slept on the side near the door but instinctively turned to look at her. She was sitting up and pointing toward the doorway. I looked into the hallway and saw what looked like a black shaggy face. It gave me a chill as I felt Carol grab my arm.

I instinctively commanded, "In the name of Jesus, be gone from our presence."

It, whatever it was, was instantly gone.

"What was it?" Carol asked.

"I have no idea," I responded. "Let's go see the kids."

We went into the kids' bedroom and looked them over. They were sleeping and had no idea as to what may have happened. We went to the landing where we saw the object. There was no evidence that anything had been there.

"Where did it go?" asked Carol.

"Downstairs, I guess." was my reply.

"Stop it! That was scary," she insisted.

"How would I know where it went? I don't know where it came from," I replied.

"Go downstairs and look," Carol insisted.

I went down and looked around, but there was nothing. I came back up the stairs, and Carol was still standing on the landing.

"Nothing," I stated as I returned.

"If that happens again, I am not going to live here," Carol commanded.

"I guess it was just a little spook that got lost," I joked.

"It's not funny," she insisted angrily.

"I know," I offered.

"It didn't have any feet or legs, did it?" she asked.

"I don't know. I saw the floor under it," I explained. "It looked like a shaggy, hairy head with two eyes. Its eyes looked mean. Let's go to sleep. Everything is fine now."

"I am not sleeping, she insisted.

"I am. God will protect us," I concluded.

The night concluded, and the next day was work as usual. When we went to bed, we made it a specific point that nothing would enter our home to harm us or scare us. We only want God's presence and protection. I have often prayed late into the night. This was a night I thought I would do just that. Even the nights that I prayed most of the night, I am not tired the next day. I do, however, ask God to let me not be tired. I lay in bed and usually only get up each hour or two.

I had been praying for about an hour when the room seemed to get lighter, but I was looking down at myself and Carol sleeping. It seemed a bit odd. I don't think I could have even thought about how this would have looked like if I could envision this sight. I went around the top of the room a couple of times, and then I was outside of the house, looking at the ground.

"See all that I shall show you," some voice commanded.

I was surprised to be looking at the snow-covered ground at about twenty feet high. I looked around to see where the voice came from when I felt a surge as if some energy was moving me. Still, I couldn't see what made this happen. I quickly saw the ocean for an instant. I thought ocean only because we were up so high, and it was so vast. I was then going over a land mass.

The voice called, "The land of the dark people."

No wind, and we had moved a vast distance so quickly. I couldn't comprehend the speed. No wind and no cold. The voice moved me over much sand and dryness. He brought me face to face with angry people. They had guns and machetes. I was scared because I was right in the middle of them.

"Fear not, for they cannot see you," the voice instructed. "We are separated by a veil."

There was much yelling. They were very angry, and they chopped at each other with their machetes. They were fighting among themselves and arguing about some others.

The voice quickly moved me to a small town. It was empty and desolate. It was of bitter smoke and many dead people.

"Know the smell," the voice commanded.

We were somehow invisible and moved quickly to another city. I came face to face with many people who were starving. We went among them. There were hundreds of thousands. There were people as far as the eye could see. We went down close to them, so close I could have touched them, but I didn't ask because of the veil. I looked into their faces, and their eyes were blank.

Suddenly we were gone, and we were in another land of much green. The people were fat, the animals were fat, and the buildings were fat. They were fighting too. They were trying to take everything from each other.

"See the greed," the voice commanded.

Again I felt the energy of being pushed, and we were gone as quickly as we had arrived. There seemed to be no time to ask questions or see more.

We came to a land where everyone was working. They were perspiring as they toiled. They said nothing as they worked. They weren't fighting or arguing. Soon the trails of people were loading ships and planes. They carried all manner of food, clothing, and many bundles. Men, women, and children were carrying all they could. The voice pushed me close to them.

"See love, and see giving," the voice commanded.

We passed all the ships and planes quickly. The stream of ships and planes seemed endless. We came to the coast of the land I first saw. We swept over the land, but everything was dead, sandy, and dry.

"The food and supplies are coming," I said to the voice.

"It's too late," the voice commanded.

I saw all the streams of planes and ships, but they didn't seem to make it to the people who needed it.

Soon I was at home, and I was viewing myself and Carol sleeping. I was perplexed to see that. Suddenly I felt myself turning over in bed. I looked up at the ceiling and around the room. I listened for the kids and heard nothing but the silence. I got up and went downstairs. It was almost morning; I had to get some sleep. I walked around and thought about what had happened. Was it a dream? It was so real.

And it repented the LORD that he had made man on the earth, and it grieved him at his heart. (Genesis 6:6)

Forty years long was I grieved with *this* generation, and said, It *is* a people that do err in their heart, and they have not known my ways. (Psalm 95:10)

And he rode upon a cherub, and did fly: and he was seen upon the wings of the wind. (2 Samuel 22:11)

My head was swimming all day with the events of last night. Smell the death, know the fear, and see the greed. See the love and the giving? The brown people never spoke, but you could smell the sweat. Were they brown from working in the sun, or was it their nationality? It has brought tears to my eyes to see the endless supply train coming to a country, which is totally dead. I had no answers. I couldn't get last night out of my head. After work, I tried to talk to Carol about what had happened. She shrugged me off as being ridiculous.

"Remember the hairy head?" I asked. You saw that.

"I don't even want to talk about that," she replied.

I went to bed and would pray again as to what to do with this information. This was a one-time thing, and I wanted to get all the information out of it, which I could. I had been praying for about an hour, and I fell asleep.

I was floating above the bed again. I was looking down at myself and Carol sleeping. It seemed a bit odd as it had last night. I went around the top of the room a couple of times, and then I was outside of the house, looking at the ground again.

"See all that I shall show you," the voice commanded again.

I felt a surge as if some energy was moving me. Still, I couldn't see what made this happen. I saw the ocean for an instant and thought it was the coast of Africa, but I didn't really know. I was then going over land as before.

The voice called, "The land of the dark people."

The voice moved me over much sand and dryness. He brought me face to face with angry people. They had guns and machetes as before. I was again scared because I was right in the middle of them.

"Fear not, for they cannot see you," the voice instructed. "We are separated by a veil," the voice said as it had before.

There was again much yelling. It was very angry, and they chopped at each other with their machetes. The voice quickly moved me to a small town. It was empty and desolate. It was of bitter smoke and many dead people.

"Know the smell," the voice commanded as before.

We moved quickly to another city. I came face to face with many people who were starving. We went among them. There were hundreds of thousands. There were people as far as the eye could see.

"This grieves me in my heart," I told the voice. "Does no one care? Does my Father in heaven not see this?"

"Your Father in heaven has grieved since man was created," the voice instructed. "See this, and know this," the voice commanded as it had before.

Suddenly we were gone, and we were in another land of much green. The people were fat, the animals were fat, and the buildings were fat. They were fighting too. They were trying to take everything from each other.

"See the greed," the voice commanded.

Again I felt the energy of being pushed, and we were gone as quickly as we had arrived. There seemed to be no time to ask questions or see more than before.

We came to the land where everyone was working as before. They were perspiring as they toiled. They said nothing as they worked. They weren't fighting or arguing. Soon the trails of people were loading ships and planes. They carried all manner of food, clothing, and many bundles. Men, women, and children were carrying all they could. The voice pushed me close to them.

"See love, and see giving," the voice commanded.

We passed all the ships and planes quickly. The stream of ships and planes seemed endless. I tried to see where the stream of planes and ships went to, but we moved so quickly I could not. We came to the coast of the land I first saw. We swept over the land, but everything was dead, sandy, and dry.

"The food and supplies are coming," I said to the voice. "Will we be in time this time?"

"It's too late," the voice commanded.

"Say it's not too late," I begged.

Soon I was at home, and I was viewing myself and Carol sleeping. I was perplexed to see that. Suddenly I felt myself turning over in bed. I looked up at the ceiling and around the room. I listened for the kids and heard nothing but the silence. I got up and went downstairs. It was almost morning; I had to get some sleep. I walked around and thought about what had happened. Was it a dream? It was so real. It was the same twice except that I tried to ask more questions.

I made a list: See all that I show you; the land of the dark people; fear not, for they cannot see you; separated by a veil; see this, and know this; know the smell; see the greed; see love, and see giving; it's too late.

I didn't know if this would happen tomorrow night, but I wanted to be prepared. There didn't seem to be time to ask questions. I went to bed without further incident. The day came and went, but I couldn't get the visions out of my head. I was troubled by them, and I was afraid of failure. What would happen if I didn't understand this? What would happen if I didn't do what I should do? I was being very uncomfortable with God.

All the next day, I wondered if this would be another night of visions, or was this it? I went to sleep with the happenings of the last two nights still in my head. I couldn't sleep. I was restless. I wanted to see the voice and hear it once more.

Soon I drifted off, and I was again looking down at myself as I floated around the top of the room. I was anticipating when the voice would arrive. After a short moment, I was outside looking at the ground, and I could feel the energy of being moved.

"See all that I shall show you," the same voice commanded.

I felt the strength of a surge as if some energy was moving me again. I still saw nothing making it happen. I just couldn't see the voice. I saw the ocean for an instant and was then going over land, which the voice called out, "This is the land of the dark people."

The voice moved me over much sand and dryness. He brought me face to face with angry people. They had guns and machetes as before.

"Why am I seeing this?" I asked.

"You will know the season," the voice boomed.

"Don't be angry with me," I pleaded as I felt intimidated. "I am not worthy of what you show me," I again pleaded. "I am afraid of failing at what I should do."

"Walk amongst them, and know them," the voice commanded as I felt the voice set me down.

They didn't seem to know I was there. The hatred was so intense; it almost had a smell to it. A voice cried out right beside me, "Don't do this evil." A machete slashed through the air, and the man fell to the ground. Blood flew all around me, but none fell on me. They fought among themselves as to destroy themselves.

The voice quickly moved me up and moved me to the small town. It was the bitter smoke and many dead people as before.

"Know the smell," the voice commanded.

We moved quickly to another city. This time all hundreds of thousands of people were lying dead everywhere. There were numbers higher than I could imagine.

"See this, and know this," the voice commanded.

"This makes me hurt inside. It makes me grieve so that I don't think I can breathe," I told the voice.

The starving people were all dead. I cried hard with much emotion. Things were getting worse. I felt a great weakness come over me.

"Can I plead to the heavens for mercy?" I asked the voice. "Will my Father in heaven stop this?"

The voice gave me no answer. I was very distressed and made an attempt to hug the voice or have the voice hug me. I was immediately strengthened.

We came to the coast of the land of much fatness. The voice brought me close. Everything was dead, charred from burning. No grass or trees nor anything that could show life, not even buildings.

We swept over the vast land, and it was all like the first. It made me grieve again. These people had so much but shared nothing. They tried to take from each other.

"What happened here?" I asked the voice.

"The hand of the Holy of holies can give blessings or take them away," the voice boomed.

"Did my Father in heaven destroy these people?" I asked. The voice gave me no answer.

We came to the land where everyone was working as before. They were not toiling. They said nothing. They were kneeling, and their heads were bowed. They were praying. They carried nothing, and the ships and planes were doing nothing. The voice pushed me close to them.

"See love, and see giving," the voice commanded.

"Who are these brown people?" I asked.

"Put these things in your heart, and you will know the season," the voice instructed.

The words carried a different temperament than before. They weren't so commanding but more of a loving, soothing tone.

"Are you Messenger from before?" I asked. There was no answer.

Soon I was at home, and I was viewing myself and Carol sleeping.

"No, voice, talk with me," I requested.

Suddenly I felt myself turning over in bed. I looked up at the ceiling and around the room. I listened for the kids, as before, and heard nothing but the silence. I got up and went downstairs. It was almost morning. I walked around and thought about what had happened. This was just too real. It was a little different than the other two nights. I tried to go back to sleep but couldn't. I felt sad for hundreds of thousands of people I didn't know. I was sad for the starving people, the fat people, and the people who toiled to give. Tears ran freely.

I waited the next night for this to happen again, but it never happened again but had changed me for life. I had tried to talk to Carol, but it was no use. I talked to a couple of ministers from different churches, and I got the same answers: "This is not possible." "It has no meaning." "You may have had some medical reason for this."

I have kept this to myself for the next thirty-some years. I have had many dynamic things happen to me. I should have died twenty times, but God saves me always. An old woman who had less than nothing gave me a blessing when I was nine. It may very well be one of the greatest gifts I have ever received. She was a stranger, but I felt like I knew her for a long time. I only delivered a Christmas present from my aunt, but she felt like she wanted to give me something. Her old feeble hand lay upon my head, and she asked that the Holy Spirit would come upon me and protect my every step. When I was nine, I didn't know what the Holy Spirit was.

> He answereth and saith unto them, He that
> hath two coats, let him impart to him that hath
> none; and he that hath meat, let him do likewise.
> (Luke 3:11)

Love in Christ, Fred

Give Me Breath

August 2014

Thought: A letter for you with as much love as it can carry. May the Spirit of God direct you in all ways, this I pray! Let's have a testimonial story and see what we can learn about protection when we are unaware even at the doorstep of death.

To all with love,

It was an early spring day, and the mystery of the night had delivered a nice white eight inches of snow. The sun was fully shining, making the world as pure white as it could only be in a dream. There was no wind, and it almost felt balmy to clear the snow from the propane storage yard and the vehicles ready to roll for the day. To get an early start at seven o'clock was a good idea. The service calls would start about eight or nine o'clock. I personally offered twenty-four-hour service, but the co-op manager said that I didn't really need to do that. I had been at the co-op for three and a half years. The best year the co-op had ever had was a sale of 330,000 gallons of propane. I did a little over one and a half million gallons in the last year. It was just two weeks ago when two other propane providers came to the co-op and had a meeting with the manager, board members, and myself. The end result was that borders were established so I could sell in their areas. I was proud of what I had accomplished. To be the best of something in a seventy-year history felt good. I give God the credit for all of it.

The snow was removed, and I was just about ready to fill some one-hundred-pound cylinders. A radio call was coming in from the office secretary.

"Fred, do you read me, over?"

"Yes, good morning, over," I replied.

"Truman K was pushing snow this morning and hit his one-thousand-gallon propane tank. He is sure it's leaking, over," Mrs. D informed me.

"I am on my way there. I will keep you informed, over," I replied.

Customer Truman was about six miles away. He was a farmer and had a busy little place. I had often asked him to not pile snow so close to his propane tank. The tank needed to be gotten to at all times. I went through possible scenarios in my head as I drove out there. It was a thousand-gallon tank, and I had just filled it about a week ago. Had the roads been cleared of snow all the way to Truman's place? The highway was good for the first three miles. I would then go on a county road for three miles and then a short half mile on a township road. As I reached the township road, there was Truman driving back to his place with the tractor. He quite often did the township road because it usually took longer for the maintainer to get the township roads done.

I followed Truman into the dooryard and stopped about a hundred feet away from the tank. As soon as I got out of the service truck, I could smell the air filled with propane. Truman drove the tractor right up to the front of the shop, about thirty feet from the tank.

I ran toward him, shouting, "Turn off the tractor!" and turn off the tractor he quickly did so.

As I reached the tractor, he was climbing back down. "This is a very volatile situation," I expressed urgently. "You need to take your wife and just leave until you hear from me in probably several hours. If all this gas ignites, it will burn up this farmyard. The tank will not explode, but all this gas will."

"I was going to help you dig out the tank," Truman insisted as he pointed to the tank buried in the snow.

"Propane is a heavy gas, and it sits on the ground. All of this dooryard has gas sitting all over it—inside the machine shed and just everywhere. Any kind of spark will ignite all of this. From where you pushed snow, I already know you hit the tank and broke the liquid valve on the bottom. You need to leave right away," I insisted.

"What about you?" Truman asked.

"I'll pray and be careful. Is there anything turned on or running or anything that could turn on around here?" I asked.

"No lights or anything," Truman responded. "There is a heating element in the cattle yard about two hundred yards from here."

"That should be okay," I offered. "Go quickly. I don't want there to be any chance of you getting injured."

Truman grabbed my arm as in a moment of "be careful" but said nothing.

I just said, "Go quickly!"

The Truman K's were gone in minutes, and I was left to dig the tank out of its snow-impacted condition. The snow was pushed up high all around the area, creating a canyon filled with propane. Propane boils at a negative forty-four degrees. The colder it is, the more it hugs the ground. The fewer breezes, the more it hangs around. This wasn't good. If it wasn't for the ethyl mercaptan added to the propane, you wouldn't even know it was there. It has no odor in its natural state.

I continued to dig the snow away. It would take about an hour, I thought. I dug for about a half an hour, making sure I didn't hit metal or create sparks of any kind. I wanted to call the office and talk to the manager before I was out here too long.

"Fred to base, over," I radioed.

In a minute, the manager responded, "This is base, over."

"Ray, you are just the one I was looking for," I responded. "I have gallons of propane leaked out all over. The snow is pushed up all around the area and is creating an area like a lake filled with gas. I filled this tank last week, so there are about seven hundred gallons in the tank. The tank is buried, so I have to dig it out. It's pushed off the blocks on one end, but the liquid valve is on the other end. Do you have any suggestions, over?"

Ray came back with his input: "If there wasn't so much gas in the tank, I would just let it leak out. Did you clear anyone from the area, over?"

"I had Truman and missus leave," I informed Ray. "I did a check with him about any spark conditions before he left. This is an old tank and an old liquid valve. Am I going to have any issues with the valve removal and getting the slam valve to slam, over?" I asked.

After a pause, Ray responded, "It should be okay. Make sure the valve is closed if possible. Take the line off before you open the valve quickly. The valve will have to open quickly to get it to slam. Turn any fittings real slow to avoid any sparking, over."

"I will give you a call if I need more information, over," I informed.

"Be careful and God speed, over," Ray chimed.

I continued to dig toward the liquid valve at the far end of the tank. In about forty minutes, I had uncovered the liquid valve. The valve stem was slightly bent, and the liquid line to the corn dryer was broken. The only good part was the liquid valve end of the tank was still well positioned on its cement blocks. The tank wasn't going anywhere from its fallen position. I changed my gloves out for a pair of safety gloves and put on my facemask shield. I removed the broken liquid line from the liquid valve. By the time I had done that little, I noticed the breathing behind my face shield seemed nauseating. I removed the shield and used some goggles instead. It seemed better, so I continued. The valve stem was bent, so I couldn't get it to close all the way. I surely couldn't get it to open quickly. I knew there was an internal slam valve, which would close if I could get a quick opening. That wasn't going to happen.

I was going to have to take the valve directly out and fairly fast to get the slamming action I would need. I couldn't get the valve to release at its threaded position in the tank. I went and found a piece of pipe and a large pipe wrench. If I couldn't get this to budge the valve, I was out of luck.

"Father, give me strength. Protect me from that which I see and that which I don't see. In Jesus's name, I pray, amen."

I carefully put the wrench and pipe-wrench combination together as not to spark. It took a very deliberate pull to get it to release, but it did release. More liquid than before began to sputter out. I needed more protection from the splatter.

A small rubber canvas I carried behind the seat in the service truck should do the trick. I retrieved it and placed it in a good position to deflect the spray of liquid, which would soon arrive. I got a smaller wrench to be able to turn the liquid valve more quickly. I began to turn the valve out as quickly as I was able. The liquid began to roar, spray, and boil a gas vapor violently. It was unnerving, so I quickly turned the valve back in. I got out of there for a bit.

I went back by the service truck and leaned against the fender. I took a few deep breaths to find some better air.

"Father, today I live by thy hand. You give me life, and you can take it away. Take away my fear as you did for me as a child and you have often done. I ask this in the name of thy Son, Jesus Christ, amen. Let it be so."

I went directly to the valve and replaced my shield in its position. I began to turn the valve out again as quickly as possible. The liquid again began to roar, spray, and boil a gas vapor violently. It made one last roar, and the slam valve closed. I replaced the liquid valve and repaired the liquid line. A good test for leaks, and I loaded up my tools. I had just pulled out of the drive, and here came Truman back home.

In whose hand *is* the soul of every living
thing, and the breath of all mankind. (Job 12:10)

Pulling my truck over, I rolled down the window and stopped. Truman did likewise.

"You should stay away a little longer," I suggested.

"I left my wife and came back to check on you," Truman replied encouragingly.

"I am okay," I replied with a smile. "With the sun shining, the gas should dissipate in a couple of hours. There is too much danger of explosion yet. Go back to town and come back after lunch. See ya, Truman. Please keep the snow pushing away from the propane tank."

"Sorry about that," Truman said in a sheepish manner.

I started to leave but watched to see if he followed me. He did but turned off and went the opposite way from town. At least he was away from the farmyard and safe.

In about two miles of travel, it felt like I couldn't get any air. I tried to get some deep breaths, but it didn't seem to work. I was struggling to keep the truck in my lane. My eyes were starting to blur. I couldn't think. Where was I? My mind was trying to black out. The clinic, yes, the clinic. Maybe I could get help there?

I saw the corner going into town. I saw no one coming, so I went through the stop sign.

Oh, that was dangerous, I thought. *I can't drive into town. I may hurt someone.*

I pulled over to the side of the road as hard as I could.

No, I reasoned. *I am still too far away.*

I forced the truck into park. I returned to driving a bit further. It took all I could do to make that happen. I pulled into the curb hard in front of the clinic. I opened the truck door to get out and walk. I knew I was a way off yet. When my legs touched the pavement, I blacked out and fell in a heap.

O spare me, that I may recover strength,
before I go hence, and be no more. (Psalm 39:13)

When I came to, I was in the clinic on oxygen. I remember falling down but not getting up and walking into the clinic. The huge scent of propane was a clue to the doctor that I may have inhaled too much propane gas. I had replaced oxygen with propane gas. I felt dizzy and nauseated. I stayed on oxygen for about four hours.

"You are very lucky to be alive," instructed Dr. R. "You were basically suffocating slowly, probably headed for brain damage. Someone was watching out for you."

"How did I get in here?" I asked.

"You walked in and collapsed on the floor," replied Dr. R.

"I remember getting out of the pickup and falling in a heap," I replied, perplexed. "I don't remember walking anywhere."

"Well, put it this way. The door burst open like you were going to attack someone. It startled all of us as you went flying in and landed in a heap in the middle of the floor. You were definitely unconscious. It was like you were thrown through the door. You should be fine," Dr. R. encouraged with a smile. "It's your lucky day."

"I thank God for the day," I whispered.

"I will give an amen to that thought," added Dr. R.

How I got there was a mystery.

> Hide not thy face far from me; put not thy servant away in anger: thou hast been my help; leave me not, neither forsake me, O God of my salvation. (Psalm 27:9)

> Ye that fear the LORD, trust in the LORD: he is their help and their shield. (Psalm 115:11)

> Let us therefore come boldly unto the throne of grace that we may obtain mercy and find grace to help in time of need. (Hebrews 4:16)

Love in Christ, Fred

I Can't Bear It

Thought: A letter for you with as much love as it can carry. May the Spirit of God direct you in all ways, this I pray! Let's have a testimonial story and see what we can learn about continuous protection from our Father in heaven. Let's visit his creation.

To all with love,

The thought of going deer hunting was like an adrenalin rush. Perhaps I should say, "Father, show me what thy hand has done so I can feel the adrenalin rush of your creation."

I suppose most people would find it strange to go deer hunting and never actually hunt a deer. When it's nice, no bugs, there is a lot of fun out there.

I had walked about a mile back into a heavily wooded area behind my uncle's house. It was totally black. The ink of night, I sometimes thought. I knew I was getting close to the tree I wanted to climb up and sit in. In the near distance, I could hear the splash of water on the rocks in the river. I loved this area when there was no snow on the ground. I had never seen anyone back here hunting. The path I was following was an old fire trail. It had some growth but was still quite able to be navigated. I rounded a bend in the path, and suddenly there was a huge crash going through the woods. I stopped and listened as the sound dissipated into the depth of the woods. I had no idea as to what it was but that it had the size to it. I stood there for a while, staring into the ink-painted woods. I couldn't even make out the trees. Whatever went charging through the woods must have run to get away from me. Animals instinctively have their fear of man. It gave me a shudder as I thought of man as a fearful creature. *It is sad really*, I thought.

I reached the edge of the river and stared across it as to locate a large tree looming into the night sky. This would tell me to go left or right to find my birch clump. I saw the great creation of God standing alone in the short distance. It was a big old oak tree, standing alone. The rest of the vegetation was brush. Oh, some of the brush was maybe fifteen feet tall, but the big oak was at least seventy feet tall. It had been there a long time, and why no others had ever joined it over the years is unknown. Vegetation growth, I guess.

I went to the left as I thought I might. If I aligned myself with the great oak, I would be in the birch clump. I soon found the clump and positioned my Remington on my shoulder as I climbed up the birches. The clump was large and offered a nice sitting area about twelve feet off the ground. I never built anything in the woods, just used what nature provided. I readied my rifle as it sat in my lap even though I knew I wouldn't use it.

Sunlight started to break over the trees and revealed more of the nightly paint job by Jack Frost. I was quite warm from walking, but after sitting for an hour, the cold was trying to say, "I'll get you."

I saw nothing, so I decided to stretch a little. I had just settled back as I picked up on a couple of small chirps from some birds in the near distance. You can go from total silence and the black of night into a new daily creation. I often thought of it as the hand of God waving over the woods and giving new life. The nighttime has to flee from light. The birds give a chirp in honor of God giving them another day. As the sun came up higher, more birds could be heard. A couple of blue jays now sounded in the distance.

> In the beginning God created the heaven
> and the earth. And the earth was without form,
> and void; and darkness *was* upon the face of the
> deep. And the Spirit of God moved upon the face

of the waters. And God said, Let there be light: and there was light. And God saw the light, that *it was* good: and God divided the light from the darkness. (Genesis 1:1–4)

My eye caught a glimpse of movement farther downstream. I remained motionless as my heart started to race. I watched closely as the object moved ever so slowly. I could now see that it was a deer and of fair size. It was still quite away from me, so the details were vague. It was moving slowly toward me. The breeze was blowing into my face, so the deer would probably not pick up on my scent. I was also a fair distance above the animal. I felt like I could hear my heart pounding as I took a slow deep breath. I was trying to relax, but I was excited. I could now see that it was a buck—and a big one too. It was about forty feet away and still coming directly toward me.

The big buck had stopped and was staring back over its shoulder into the woods. I knew at any time it could just flee. The thought came into my mind of shooting the big buck. I readied my rifle but kept it on my lap. I wanted to bring it to position to shoot if I made the decision to take the deer. The buck dropped its head and sniffed the ground. It continued to do so as it moved even closer to my position. It was now about twenty feet away. It was moving very slow and then stopping. I started to count the points on its rack. It looked like fifteen or sixteen points. This was the biggest rack I had ever seen this close in the wild.

"I don't really want to shoot you, but I may just have to," I whispered.

It stopped and looked back into the woods. Had it heard me whisper? It went back to sniffing the ground and came right under my tree. I raised the rifle and aimed at the great animal. *Click,* the rifle went. The great buck was gone in three leaps with its white flag fully extended. I must have accidentally hit the release on the pump stock and release the firing pin enough to keep it from discharging the shell. I laughed.

What a thrill, I thought. I couldn't be happier. What a hunter I am.

I slowly climbed down out of my birch clump. I was stiff and a bit chilled, so I thought I would move around a bit. I had wanted to explore an old road on the south edge of town. It had been a well-used road many years ago. It was about a mile away as the crow flies, so I cut across the old vacated meadow at an angle. The tall grasses were well to my shoulders. It offered a different type of walk as it crunched beneath my feet. It brushed on by me with little resistance. It just offered a shushing sound to say hello. It was more like early October than November. There had been a heavy frost overnight, but the sun had wiped it away.

As I came near the wooded area, a moist scent filled the air with wet leaves. I took in a deep breath to get the most of the smell. I pushed my way through forty feet of brush and trees. A small climb through a shallow ditch, and I was up on the old dumping ground road. Years ago every little town had a dumping ground. The residents would take their trash, scraps, and other unwanted items out to these sites and discard them. Back in the day, I would visit these sites with my uncle—this one in particular as he lived in this small town. He would collect the scrap metal, wire, and resalable items. It was sometimes a gold mine of wonderful items. To find a lawn-mower, bicycle, washer, engine that you could repair made it very worthwhile. A worker would come out and burn the unwanted ever so often. A hole would be dug, and ash would be buried. Now the old road was forgotten. The road was now only traveled by adventure seekers such as me. I observed the sandy road for recent tracks, but there were none to be found. It seemed forgotten as I looked back over my shoulder to see my tracks in the sandy soil. When mankind finds no value, he moves on. God sweeps his hand over the forgotten and gives it back to nature.

The road went straight to an old bridge, which crossed the river or turned a small bend in the road to enter the old dumping ground area. I followed the bend. It revealed a large area in which nature had taken back. I walked a good distance to where the back of the old dumping ground would have ended. If you could look underground, you would find evidence, I am sure, but not on top. The only evidence of man was my footprints in the sandy soil. I walked through a clump of pines and soon found myself in heavy brush.

"This is no good," I whispered.

I decided to turn around and walk back out. I would go back to the road and walk a bit further to the old bridge and see if it is still there.

Out of the brush through the clump of pines, and I froze. About thirty yards away was a huge black bear. It stood there staring at me and me staring at it. It was jet black, but its face had considerable graying. It stayed on all four feet, its ears turned a little this way and that. I could see it move its nose as it tried to sniff me out. It rose up partway and went back down. My heart had gone from a calm beat to beating out of my throat. When I was seven, I had been twenty feet from a black bear, but it was on the other side of a barb wire fence and tall brush. I didn't recall being scared then, but now it seemed so different. I didn't bring my rifle up nor twitch a muscle.

The bear took a couple of steps forward and rose up partway again. I wondered why it didn't seem to sense me. Was it too old? Could it not see well? It knew I was something. It was quite close to town and probably was not too afraid of people. The great bear rose all the way up onto its hind legs. It made a strange puffing sound. The bear may have a grayed face, but it was of massive size. It was about five of me. The great beast was maybe eight feet tall or more and maybe six hundred pounds. Was the beast headed somewhere to hibernate? It pawed at me with its left paw. It made a couple of more puffing sounds and dropped to its four feet and slowly turned to its right and walked into the woods. "Thank you, Father, for your protection," I whispered. This is the second time I know that I have encountered a bear, which could have eaten my lunch.

I stayed where I was for another ten minutes. I slowly walked to where the bear had been standing. I knelt down to observe the great paw prints. I laid my hand inside of a track. It was pressed into the sand, but it took about three of my hands to equal the size. I traced the paw print with my finger. I could see where there were claw markings on some of the tracks. I stood up and followed the path where I had come in on. The tracks of the great beast were right on top of mine. I followed the tracks all the way back to where I had come up out of the small ditch. The bear had picked up on my trail in the woods or perhaps in the vacated meadow. It gave me a chill at the thought of the great beast tracking me.

I continued on my journey toward the old bridge. I thought about the great bear and wondered if it had lived its whole life around the dumping ground. We had seen bears at the various dumps before. People would skin out fish and throw table scraps in their trash.

It would be good food for a bear, I thought.

I was no longer anxious about the bear but in marvel of the great beast. I would probably never have another such encounter. I am not sure that I would want to. It was a great adventure, but it could have gone in many other directions. Some of the possibilities may not have been so good. It reminded me of my punishment for not running to the house when I was seven.

I reached the old bridge to find it in bad condition. Most of the frames across the river were still in place, but the rails and deck planks were gone. Perhaps someone had come out here years ago and stripped off some of the materials. I sat down on the edge and listened to the water on the rocks. I threw a pebble in the water every so often. I had never been beyond the old bridge, so I couldn't really speculate as to where the old road went to. Again mankind had no use, so God would sweep his hand over the land and take it back.

Love in Christ, Fred

Deer Me

October 2014

Thought: A letter for you with as much love as it can carry. May the Spirit of God direct you in all ways, this I pray! Let's have a testimonial story and see what we can learn about continuous protection from our Father in heaven.

To all with love,

The thought of going deer hunting was like an adrenalin rush. You may be thinking already of deer hunting as the shooting of a deer for food or sport. You wouldn't be wrong about traditional deer hunting, but my deer hunting has never yielded the death of a deer by my hand. My hunting was visiting relatives in Northern Minnesota. It was a trek into the woods and finding that spot where perhaps no one had gone to. I enjoyed this area as a child and missed it when we left the area. Missing it felt like a goose going north or south during migration. Few people realize how much enjoyment is in the wilderness. The incident should be about spring, but instead, it's the first week of November.

Traditional deer hunting has a tradition of starting before sunrise. This one would be no different as I arrived at a favorite uncle's house in the little town of Hubbard, Minnesota. It was a small town of less than a hundred people. The sleepy little town by Long Lake didn't seem to ever change. Nothing new seemed to get built, and no one seemed to add changes to their properties. The fun little store in the center of town had been started by Leonard when he returned from the Navy during World War II. He only wanted to make enough to live and no more. He said it was the most peaceful life he could ever imagine. He loved the town, the lake, and the big trees. My uncle and aunt also settled there at the same time—they were always great friends—to float in a boat that you used oars to navigate. The large sleepy lake they loved to fish in was hypnotizing. You could easily fall asleep in the little boat as you fished. Perhaps it was a day for a picnic under the big pines. The sweet evergreen aroma was also peaceful. Who says fifty-, sixty-, or seventy-year-old people don't go on picnics? You are really missing out if you don't go on a real picnic.

I arrived late in the evening on a very warm November day. The week saved up for vacation was going to be well worth it. It was always the first week of November, and you never knew what you were going to get. This was usually a colder time of the year. There wasn't a hint of snow anywhere. The ground was filled with dry and colorful leaves. I thought I was going to be in heaven as I drove up in front of the little three-room light-blue house tucked in the edge of the woods. My uncle greeted me at the door as it was their friendly way to do so. My aunt had passed away several years ago, so that part was a little sad. What better reason to show up for a friendly visit? They had no children of their own so you felt like the adopted child. They offered more love than most families. With some quick help of carrying the groceries in I always brought, it was the invite for supper. We are having beef stew. Oh, yum! The savory taste of beef stew is so good.

The next morning early with the blackness of the night still showing itself, we prepared the traditional breakfast of eggs, bacon, hash browns, toast, and coffee. The wonderful smell would quickly fill the small house. A good conversation and some hardy laughs brought about the time to go. A small homemade bag of trail mix was tucked into the overall pocket. Though I carried a rifle and extra shells, I have never shot a deer in my life. A hardy greeting to return and see you for lunch, and I was off. You wanted to find a spot in the woods and stay put as not to disturb anyone else who may be out for a hunt. I would drive a couple of miles out of town and walk back into the woods, where I knew there wouldn't be many, if anyone, hunting.

I pulled into a field drive and parked on the edge of a field. This was nice to not have any snow. There was a little frost, but it felt like the beginning of a great day. I soon found an old familiar fire trail that I knew would run for miles into the woods. I knew that deer like to run on this small, rarely used path as much as I did. In a few hundred yards, there was a very large log, about two feet in diameter and perhaps twelve feet long. I would peer through the darkness for it and find a nice spot to sit beside it. I really wanted that spot because of all the leaves on the ground. I had been walking down the path for a while.

I should have been there by now, I thought. *Had I missed it?*

I would go a bit further and then I would backtrack. There was a small clump of oak trees in this area. There were maybe twelve to fifteen big oak trees.

It should be easy to find them even in the dark, I thought.

The sweet scent of the pines was distracting me, I contemplated. Ah, at last, the big oaks. I hadn't missed them. The big long was just about ten feet off the path on the south side. I quickly found my old friend the log. It probably had been lying on the forest floor for thirty or forty years. It had probably been growing in this area for maybe another 150 years, so a quiet "How are you, my old friend?" was warranted. You could clear your head here and enjoy nature or talk to God. The spirit of God is everywhere if you want to listen.

This was fun as I settle down into a deep drift of leaves. I knew this was going to be perfect. I leaned my rifle against the log with no intention of using it even though it was cleaned and loaded. I had to wear the orange vest as it was the law. I guess it would help me from accidentally being shot.

I sat very still and listened for sounds. It was so quiet. Not even a peep from a bird. The sun was getting close to the horizon as a grey color started to replace the inky black of night. The areas that the white frost could get to helped to lighten things up.

Crack, crack.

Two large dry branches snapped a short distance away from me. I turned my head slowly toward where the sound came from. I knew that whatever it was, it was large.

A person, a large deer, a bear, or perhaps a wolf, I wondered.

There was a very light air current from the direction of where the sound came from, so whatever it was, it would probably not smell me.

The sun just broke the horizon, and the light came shooting through the trees. It started to lighten up in a hurry now. A few blue jays made their common call in the distance. It felt like home as I listened to the sound. I continued to search in the distance where I had heard the braches break a few moments ago. Whatever it was, it was so gone by now. No, wait! My mind rushed for a moment. I was seeing the most beautiful whitetail deer which I had ever seen. Most whitetails are a dark brown-gray mix, even some blackish mixes. This deer had a total head-to-hoof light, sweet-brown coat. The bright white underbelly and under tail seemed enhanced. This was so light of brown, as the color of clay. It was a doe of about medium age, I guessed. It was quite large for a female whitetail. I will call her the queen of the whitetails.

She had no clue that I was even there. She was not more than fifty feet away. I could have easily shot her, but I wouldn't. There were minimal trees between us, and she kept looking the other way back into the woods. She twitched her ears, straightened her ears, and listened. She took a couple of slow steps. The sunlight hit her coat and made a bright, brassy gleam.

"May you have many fawns as beautiful as you," I whispered.

She may have heard my whisper as she turned her head and looked in my direction. Deer have very good hearing. Her white tail came up halfway and stopped. She stopped her left front hoof once. Her tail came up all the way, and she trotted away. She knew something wasn't right but didn't know what, or she would have just flown out of the area. The most beautiful light-cinnamon-colored deer—not a blemished color anywhere on her. Thank you, Father!

I sat there for perhaps a half hour when suddenly I heard the sound of hooves running down the frozen path I had walked in on.

An eight-point buck was flying down the path at full speed. I saw him coming, and then I saw him going. He didn't have a clue that I was there. His tail was up, and he was fleeing from danger. He was caught out in the open after sunup and was probably headed to a slew area that was farther down the path. I had been there many times before. It was almost mystic back there in the swampy area. The grass would be six or eight feet tall even this time of the year. It was a great place for whitetails.

I waited to see if any hunters came walking down the path looking for the big buck. Nothing happened, and all was quiet. An occasional crow would break the silence. I would visit the swamp perhaps tomorrow and see the ancient blue spruce trees. They were so old and so grand. You couldn't put your arms halfway around them. They were maybe 150 years old.

It was time for a stretch, so I stood up. I had been sitting for a couple of hours. I leaned back against the big log and pulled the small bag of trail mix from my pocket. It was a mix of raisins, sunflower seeds, peanuts, and a few almonds. It was all quite tasty. I had a zip pocket by my lower thigh in my overalls with a bottle of water tucked away, so I had a drink of water. A squirrel jumped off one of the oaks on the far edge of the oak clump. He started digging around under the leaves. You couldn't see the squirrel, but you could see the leaves popping up in the air magically. It was funny and had my attention for five or ten minutes until it came back out and jumped back onto the base of the oak. It seemed to have its mouth stuffed full of something. I guessed it was stuffed full of acorns. This was a banquet area for squirrels and deer. They both love acorns.

This was such a nice place as it beckoned me to stay longer. I began raking the leaves into a pile where I had been sitting. In a short time, I was kicking up acorns. I sat down in my pile of leaves and picked up an acorn. I opened it with my knife and ate the acorn. It was a meaty nut, but it didn't tempt me to eat another. I do think it was good food for a squirrel. That was what the squirrel had in its bulging mouth.

The sun was making it so comfortable I was getting sleepy. A comfortable leafy pile, a warm sun, a sweet pine scent, and a few blue

Jays sounding in the distance, and I dozed off. I woke up with the sound of a snapping branch behind me. I didn't move but listened intently. I could hear something moving in the leaves on the other side of the big log. It sounded small, so I thought it was the squirrel. It was scraping on the other side of the log. I remained motionless because I didn't want to scare it away. No matter what it was, it seemed to like scraping on the log.

I started to turn my head to the left as I heard it making more noise to that side. I had just turned my head when I saw two tiny hoofs coming over the log. The next thing I saw was two big dark eyes looking straight at me about two feet away. It was the tiniest fawn I had ever seen. It now was lying over the top of the big log. Its feet were way off the ground. It just let its body hang over the log and stared at me. I moved a little, and it made no motion of being afraid.

"What are you trying to do?" I asked. "Do you not have any concept of walking around the log? You are all hung up right now."

It was so small. It was such a beautiful light brown with a fill of white spots. I don't know if it weighed twenty-five pounds.

"Where is your mother?" I asked. "Why were you born so late in the fall? You have your seasons all goofed up. I am sorry to say life is going to be hard for you. I hope your mother is around. You most defiantly need her."

I reached over slowly and touched it on the nose. A little pink tongue came out and tried to suck my finger. I let it for just a minute. It was hungry. I pulled my finger back. It began to rock its body back and forth on the log. It was trying to get out of its predicament. Soon it toppled over the log and landed beside me. It pulled its feet under and curled up a bit to just lay there. It seemed content to just lay there. It knew I was something but had no fear of what I was. I just sat there and watched the fawn breathe slowly. I neither heard nor saw any other deer. It stayed there for about twenty minutes. I prayed for the little fawn. I had never prayed for an animal before.

"Dear heavenly Father, I know that you know all creatures. I know you see this small fawn, which was born out of season. Let it live. Help it to live and enjoy the life you have let it have. Some may think this is a strange thing to pray about. At this moment in time, you have given me a wonderful experience, which will last all my life. You are so good to me. I thank you for this wonderful day. It's in Jesus's name I ask this."

The fawn had its eyes closed and was breathing contently. I didn't want to leave my scent on the fawn, but it was so tempting to want to touch it. I had to let that temptation pass. In a couple of minutes, it lifted its head and then rose to its feet. It looked at me and turned away. It started to walk away. It was so small, so it was not surprising that a few steps didn't get it very far. I watched as it came up to a very small clump of brush. It leaned into the bush to push itself through it. It seemed determined to go in a given direction as if it knew where it wanted to go. I really don't think it had a clue. It was just going in a direction.

The small encounter made me think. Do we really know where we are going? Are we just going in a direction? Are we maybe as helpless as this small fawn and just don't realize it just as that fawn doesn't realize it? Father, did you put this fawn here in this place and time for me? This was very strange to me and had God's hand all over it. I will never forget this time or its meaning.

> For we know that the whole creation groaneth and travaileth in pain together until now. (Romans 8:22)

> I have no greater joy than to hear that my children walk in truth. (3 John 1:4)

Love in Christ, Fred

Deer, Cousin Bill

November 2014

Thought: A letter for you with as much love as it can carry. May the Spirit of God direct you in all ways, this I pray! Let's have a testimonial story and see what we can learn about witnessing anywhere.

To all with love,

I had been working on a general livestock farm for the last six years in Iowa. The two brothers I was working for decided to split up, so that left us out. My wife was all upset about it, but I assured her everything would be fine.

"How you can say such a thing," she replied. "We have no prospects, we have three children, and we have no money."

"We have $2,000, and we are capable of working. Where do you want to live?" I asked.

Her reply was to move back to Minnesota to be close to her parents. I know such things are more stressful for some folks, and all I wanted was for her and the kids to be happy. For me, as always, God was everything; and for her, it was "How can you talk about God at a time like this?"

We moved back to the small town of Sherburn, Minnesota. We moved into a small three-room apartment for $125 a month. We got moved in, and I walked across the street to a local co-op for a job.

I was told that the LP gas technician was leaving next week and if I could do the job.

I replied, "I surely can do the job, and God will help me with whatever I need to know."

The old manager sat back in his chair and stared at me for a moment. "That's an interesting answer," he finally responded. "You can start Monday."

My wife was all happy—temporarily. In two months we had moved into a house. I had to do some part-time work along the way, but I didn't mind it as long as I could go back to Northern Minnesota and see some relatives and go deer hunting, it's all good.

"It's cold and miserable. Why go?" was the send-off response. "It's the first week of November, and you have no choice."

I was off to the north. The little $600 pickup rattled down the road, but I was pleased to have it. I knew money was tight—always. I had $200 for my trip, so it had to be enough. It was going to be a cold week, but I was drawn to do this. I knew I would probably not shoot a deer, for my purpose was going into the wilderness to talk to God and see his creation of nature. I knew most people, including my wife, couldn't understand this.

I arrived at my destination with warm greetings from my aunt and uncle.

"We have missed you so and love you more than we can say. You couldn't talk your wife into coming?"

"No, I spent most of the year trying to convince her, but it was like inviting her to go to Siberia."

This aunt and uncle had no children of their own. They had a girl that was born within one day of my birth and sadly didn't live. I was treated like a shared child. The visit was like a year in the making. My aunt was blind for several years now but never reflected that it was any kind of handicap.

"It's miserably cold. Are you going to hunt?" my aunt asked.

"Oh yes, but perhaps not for long periods of time," I replied.

"We already have six or seven inches of snow. It is supposed to snow hard tomorrow," my uncle added.

"I will wait for light before I go out. Just better visibility," I suggested. "We will have more time to play cards," I joked.

It was snowing hard the next morning when I set off. I had another uncle a few miles out of town. My aunt and uncle had a small farm and some wooded land. They were gone on a road trip with their truck and wouldn't be back for a few more days. I would park in their yard and go walking. As I entered the wooded area, the snow and wind didn't seem to find me. The woods went for about three-quarters of a mile before it dumped into a slew and then into the river. The wind chill was twenty-five below zero this morning, but it didn't seem bad in the trees. It was quiet except for the wind over the treetops. I hadn't seen anyone in town or on the road out here. My aunt and uncle that owned this property were the only people within about four miles. I was wondering where all the animals were as I walked along slowly. They no doubt had found somewhere to hide from the storm. There was enough snow on the forest floors to walk very quietly. Every time I came across a tight clump, I investigated it for life.

I saw a small clump of blue spruce ahead, about fifty feet away. They were only four to six feet tall but very thick. Maybe twenty small trees, I guessed.

I was about fifteen feet away when a large doe jumped out of the clump. It startled me as I froze my movement. She stopped her flight in about forty feet. The doe was of unusual color. Its light-cinnamon color was total and complete from head to toe. The under neck, underbelly, and under tail were of the purest white. She just stood there for me to take in my fill of her beauty. She was quite large for a doe. Most whitetails are smaller and kind of a dirty gray-brown mix. I had a rifle and could probably shoot her easily, but I had no intention of doing so. I was going to stand there until she decided to go. After several minutes, she trotted off toward the river. I didn't know it at the time, but I would see her three years later or at least an exact replica.

The little clump of blue spruce looked inviting. I went into the clump and sat down. It was indeed the perfect little nest for a deer. It even had a nice pine scent. I pulled out some trail mix and just sat for a while. I suppose I left my scent in the nest so she may not return to this place for some time, I thought. I decided to keep moving to prevent it from getting cooled down.

I soon saw the slew in the distance. I knew it would be frozen over. That would be the only way to walk it, and I had never had the chance before. You would always break through and make it impossible to investigate. There were hundreds of clumps of rushes. *Surely deer would like this place*, I contemplated.

I began walking around the outside of the slew. I went very slowly so that I may have a chance to find a deer hiding. I had gone maybe 150 yards; I had no sight of anything

All of a sudden, there was a loud bang on my right side. It caught me so by surprise I stumbled to my left. My first thought was that my rifle had fired. No, it hadn't. I turned slightly and saw a hunter come out of a small clump of pines, maybe five or six pines, about ten feet, away.

"Sorry about that, old boy," he replied. "I saw a deer move in that clump of rushes just there," he instructed as he pointed ahead about twenty feet.

"It just startled me, cousin," I replied.

"Are you my cousin?" the man asked.

"Maybe in some ways. I just use the term now and again," I informed the hunter.

"I'm Bill," the hunter introduced himself.

I pulled my glove off and introduced myself as, "Fred. This is my uncle's land."

"Oh, Marlin is your uncle. I know him well," Bill instructed.

We walked over to the clump of rushes.

"That's the biggest, beefiest buck with the smallest rack I have ever see," Bill laughed.

"I was thinking the same thing," I returned. "It's only four points, and maybe the rack is the size of my hand. How come it's so beefy?" I asked.

"Eating your uncle's corn, I guess," Bill suggested. "I guess genetics and not running after any does," Bill laughed. "Do you want half?"

"No, but I will help you drag him out," I offered.

"Man, I needed this deer," Bill said in an appreciative manner as he cut a three-foot piece of heavy branch. We placed the branch under the deer's chin and tied it with a small rope.

"It sure is a nice color," I inserted.

"Yea, cinnamon," Bill replied. "It's a rare color for a whitetail."

The deer was going to be a hard haul, I realized as we started to pull it.

"I wish I had a four-wheeler," Bill said hopefully. "Crap, I wish I had a job. It seems like everything is seasonal or part-time. Lori, my wife, is on me all the time to look. She works as a fast-food clerk. We have a four-year-old boy by the name of Jason."

"I have three little girls and live in Southern Minnesota. I am just here visiting my relatives," I offered in return.

"If you hadn't come along when you did, I was just about to leave," Bill informed me.

I was near frozen.

"I don't think I could have gotten this monster out of here. I would have to have cut it up and carried it a little at a time. The cupboard is pretty bare. Lori thought I was nuts to go hunting, but it only lasts a week. I told her I am doing my best or bust. She is going to be so happy. She may not say so much if I have a couple of beers."

I was just letting Bill talk away.

"Let's rest a minute?" he asked.

"Sure," I replied.

"I feel like I took this deer away from you," Bill said in an apologetic manner.

"Well, consider it a gift," I replied with a laugh. "I go deer hunting for the feel of the woods, to visit relatives, and to talk to God."

"Yea, well I don't talk to God."

"How come?" I asked.

"My parents never do," Bill responded. "Nor my grandparents or any relatives go to church or talk to God."

"Mine either," I returned.

"Why you then?" Bill asked.

"Let's pull some more," I suggested. "It's like this deer, Bill," I started. "I can't make a deer. You need the deer for food."

"Boy, do I?" Bill inserted. "I can't work hard enough to live. If the cupboard is bare, Lori gets in a panic. Then we find everything to complain about."

We pulled for a while in silence.

"Let's rest," Bill requested.

"So let's say you would have left your spot and went home, Bill," I reiterated. "No deer, bare cupboard, mad or sad Lori, and just no fun. Instead, you have a big deer—a bigger deer than you hope to have gotten. I just happened to walk by at the right time, a well-below-zero day, and everything is trying to hide. We are probably the only two whacko cousins out hunting. This is probably only one of a couple of deer even in this area right now. Don't you think for even a minute that there is a little credit due somewhere?"

"Yea, you, cousin," Bill replied. "You are the man of God."

I laughed as I said, "Just call me Fred or cousin. Let's say we give God just a little credit even if you don't believe in him."

"If you look at it that way, you kind of want to believe," Bill replied with a shuffle in the snow. "Let's pull again."

The task at hand was just that as we continued in silence.

"What would I do if I wanted to believe like you?" Bill asked as the silence was broken.

"I have gone through a lot of trials in my short life so far," I answered Bill. "It's not always easy. Even though I don't have supportive relatives, God usually inserts someone into my life as assistance. The one thing that always helps me is John 3:16 through 19 in the Bible."

I recited it to Bill:

> For God so loved the world that he gave his only begotten Son, that whosoever believeth in him should not perish, but have everlasting life. For God sent not his Son into the world to condemn the world; but that the world through him might be saved. He that believeth on him

is not condemned: but he that believeth not is condemned already, because he hath not believed in the name of the only begotten Son of God. And this is the condemnation, that light is come into the world, and men loved darkness rather than light, because their deeds were evil. (John 3:16–19)

"See, most people put the word *God* on a shelf and don't want to look any further. It's easy to take what you want, do what you want, and maybe only think about your immediate family. It is the natural part of man to do all the bad stuff. If man had no laws, what do you think he would do? The most powerful would get everything, and the rest would just die. Now if everyone believed in God and the son we just spoke of, what would be the difference? No one would want anything. Let's say you give up just one purchase of beer and took the money and gave it to Lori—like flowers or something she likes. Lori doesn't drink beer like you, Bill. So you don't have to quit beer cold turkey, but give something of you to Lori or Jason—just for them—and what would you see?"

"Shock for sure," Bill replied. "I haven't given flowers forever. She might cry, and for sure there would be hugs coming my way."

"Always think of giving and not what you may or may not receive," I added. "Then your mom and dad—do something for them."

"I don't have a dad," Bill inserted.

"Then your mother will appreciate it that much more," I suggested. "Your life will change just like that."

"Let's rest again," Bill requested.

We knelt in silence for a moment as Bill pulled around on the small set of antlers.

"So I believe God sent his Son into the world to take away all my bad stuff. I give up something that is of me?" Bill asked.

"It's a beginning," I agreed. "See Jesus, the son of God, came into this world, never sinned, and died on a cross by the hand of man. He went into hell, but hell couldn't contain him, and he ascended into heaven. He is the only way to get to the Father for salvation. Salvation is the chance to live with God forever. Surprise Lori with an offer to go to church, and just check out what you may be missing. It's a learning growing process. I think if you find a good church, you will also find help if you need it. Maybe it's someone to talk to, a bag of groceries, help to do a job that's too big for you."

"Let's pull again," Bill requested.

The destination was finally reached. We lifted with a struggle to get the beast into the old Chevy pickup.

"Look at the size of this deer," Bill laughed. "You sure you don't want some?"

"No, the gift is all yours, Bill."

Bill removed his glove and held out his hand. I did likewise no matter how cold it was.

"Cousin, man of God, Fred, or whoever you are, you are strange. But I wished you lived next door. I couldn't forget this day if I tried. I am going to try to do what you told me." Bill saluted.

"I will never forget you, Bill. I pray God will bless you and keep you."

As I watched Bill drive away, I whispered, "Father in heaven, I have been deer hunting today. Thank you, I have enjoyed it. I see why it had to be so cold today."

Love in Christ, Fred

2014 Christmas Story
The Most Important Thing

December 2014

Thought: A letter for you with as much love as it can carry. May the Spirit of God direct you in all ways, this I pray! Let's have a testimonial story and see what—say what? It's time for a Christmas story?

To all with love,

Christmas was just a few days off with crispness in the air and the white billows of new snow everywhere. The big flakes of snow were gently falling with no hint of wind it seemed almost magical. Work still had to be done as I forced the gas truck down the road. Mrs. Johanson was on today's delivery list, but she always wanted me to call her Isabelle. It was always pleasant to stop and fill Isabelle's propane tank, I thought as I downshifted to enter her dooryard. Pulling into the short driveway, I noticed all the snow clinging to the tree branches. The branches were canopying over the lane and adding to the magic of the season. The twenty-acre-thick grove held its own mystery as Mr. and Mrs. Johanson had never wanted to change it. It was their sanctuary, and all that lived within the beautifully wooded area found safety.

The tank was filled, and the ticket was produced and added to my pocket. I grabbed the shovel off the truck and began to clear the sidewalk to the house. By the time I reached the steps, I could hear the door inside the porch creaking open. I knew about how much time I had to finish as it took Isabelle a long time for her ninety-seven-year body to reach the door. I had told her many times she didn't have to greet me at the door, but she insisted. I finished and had the outside door open with one step in, and the door closed before she had crossed the porch floor.

I enjoyed sounding off a "Merry Christmas" as it was the season for merriment. Isabelle sounded a "Merry Christmas" back with a smile and a twinkle of her blue eyes. I put my hand on her arm and helped her do an about-face and return to inside the house. I noticed it was quite dark and cold in the house and questioned why it was so. Isabelle replied that it had been like this since yesterday. She slowly explained that she thought it was the fuse box giving her the problem. There was a fuse box on the third floor, which was the attic. Isabelle pointed to the flashlight on the kitchen table and put her hand on my arm with an added caution to be careful as I climbed the many steps to the attic.

With my reassurance returned to Isabelle, I opened the door to the upstairs and started the ascent. It was difficult to find enough room for a single step at a time. Books were stacked about two feet tall on either side of every step. I knew that Isabelle liked to read and had many books, but what I saw was beyond my wildest expectations. I had never been beyond the kitchen nor living room as it was the only area of the home in which she used. She had many years of teaching school, and that was the start of this accumulation. Isabelle had started teaching school when she was sixteen. She married shortly after and outlived her husband as well as her children. This big old house had been her home for over eighty years.

My thoughts were reflecting the many things she had told me over the years when my hand touched feather rather than each pile of books I had been navigating. It startled me as I whipped the flashlight around to view what the feathers I touched were. Staring back at me was a two-foot-tall stuffed blackbird. It looked so alive even if it was stuffed. It appeared to be some kind of eagle.

The stairs were longer than normal due to the twelve-foot room ceilings. I continued up the second flight of stairs and finally reached the attic. I quickly sorted through the fuse panel and the extra fuses that were left for spares. As I was instructed by Isabelle, I pulled a string on a light nearby to test for electricity to see if it had returned. The light came on, so I knew some of the electricity had returned. I was hoping the second fuse I had found would return power to the heater in the living room. With a creepy return by the bird on the stair, I was soon returning to the living room. I heard the heater running as I returned and proceeded to the light switch by the door for a test. The light came on, and all seemed well.

Isabelle came shuffling across the floor and open her arms for a hug. I returned the compliment even when her hug seemed to not stop.

"I am so happy! You made my Christmas" she whispered.

"I just replaced a couple of fuses," I replied with a hand gesture added.

"To me heat and lights are everything," she replied sternly. Come over and see my tree."

The small table by the sofa held a little tree. It was about eighteen inches tall and held a few small wooden ornaments.

"Sit for a minute and have a cookie," she said hopefully. She explained that the neighbors who rented her farm had brought over some Christmas cookies. She told me how wonderful the cookies were. She had eaten her first half cookie this morning and would eat the other part as I had my cookie.

Isabelle explained how her husband, Carl, had carved the wooden ornaments over many years. It was the labor of love over many years that made the tree come to life. She had always had a real tree each year. I reached over and touched the small tree and found out it was real. I leaned closer and had a smell of its rich evergreen fragrance.

"Where did the small tree come from?" I inquired.

Isabelle responded that she had gone out to the edge of the woods and cut it down with a meat cleaver. It had taken a good part of a day, but it was sunny and worth every minute.

I responded that she could call me if she needed help. She tried to assure me, that she was very capable but quite slow.

"Is the little tree really that important?" I asked.

Isabelle reached over and put her hand on top of mine. She smiled, and her blue eyes twinkled. "The birth of Jesus Christ is the most important thing in my life. I celebrate it every day but especially with a tree this time of year. I ask for no gifts, for I have everything I need."

(Read Luke 2:1–20—Jesus Christ's birth.)

"If you asked for a gift, what would you ask for?" I asked curiously.

Isabelle quickly responded, "May my savior Jesus Christ take me home."

> For God so loved the world, that he gave his
> only begotten Son, that whosoever believeth in
> him should not perish, but have everlasting life.
> For God sent not his Son into the world to con-
> demn the world; but that the world through him
> might be saved. (John 3:16–17)

I felt my heart swell up in my throat. I quickly informed Isabelle that I had to get back to work. I greeted her goodbye. I felt tears coming down my cheeks before I reached the truck. I cried like a baby all the way to the next customer. It was the enjoyment of her cookie, tree, and Christ in her heart.

Love in Christ, Fred

Help Me, I'm Falling

January 2015

Thought: A letter for you with as much love as it can carry. May the Spirit of God direct you in all ways, this I pray! Let's have a testimonial story and see what we can learn about continuous protection from our Father in heaven for, perhaps, witnessing to another?

To all with love,

It was always a big rush to get chores done when there were large jobs for the day to be done. This early September day was one of those days. The three hours of chores were done, and it was already close to 9:00 a.m. I had to get the blower repaired and made ready for filling the silo with corn silage. This unloading device was in the top of a 110-foot silo. This year we were renting the neighbor's silo for feeding extra cattle. The two brothers I was working for pretty much just turned me loose on anything they wanted to be done. It had already been five good years working for them. To find someone with a good Christian attitude to work for is priceless. The neighborhood all went to the same country church. We all helped each other on many different levels. It really was like a large family with each part living a half mile apart. We laughed together, played together, shopped together, and did many more wonderful things. It made you feel like you really belonged.

The blower had to be ready for use in the top of the silo before the silage reached the fullness of the silo. The silage gathered a yellow toxic gas on top of it when it was in the curing stage. The gas could overcome and kill you in minutes. You would never be able to climb back down the silo chute to safety before being overcome. Nitrogen dioxide is a toxic gas that forms in twelve to sixty hours after filling. If you fill for a day or two and stop, it's there. The best fill would be to fill and not stop until you are done and the silo is full. However, because of the sheer weight as you go up, it will compress and settle. The blower and unloading device are left off until it reaches its fullness. You will then use it to distribute the silage so as to obtain a nice even fullness.

The crisp morning would soon give way to a bright sunny day. The hint of leaves changing was here and there. Fall was saying, "I am coming."

I greeted our neighbor with a good-hearted "Good morning." He was done with his chores and offered to lower the unloading device when I was ready to do so. It would save a lot of time because it needed to be at a certain height.

"I will need about twenty minutes to get everything ready for the move," I explained. "I will shout down to you when I am ready."

The silo chute on a 110-foot silo is about three feet in diameter. The ladder rungs are larger too. They have twice as much space from the little doors they are fastened to out to the rung you climb on. The little doors are about two feet square and run all the way to the top inside the silo chute. The power for the unloading and silage distribution device is supplied by a cable, which runs up the inside of the silo chute. The cable is about one-and-a-quarter-inch in diameter and has a five-pound plug on the end for a connection to the unloading device.

I began the ascent up the ladder. "I will give you a shout in about twenty minutes," I reinstructed.

"Okay," the neighbor replied.

As I ascended, I felt a breeze flowing up the chute. It was like a little wind tunnel, I thought. I always thanked God for giving me another day. The more beautiful the day, the more you enjoy it. When you get about halfway up, you start feeling the task of the climb. I stopped for a quick breather and took a look down the chute. I could see the neighbor standing on the ground and waiting patiently. I again hurried my ascent. At last, I reached the last door. Above the last door, there was a small four-foot triangle. To stare down into the 110-foot silo could get a little dizzying if you let it. The silo was twenty-four feet in diameter. It was a monster.

First there were some stabilizing chains, which had to be moved around. There were some clamping and spout directional brackets, which had to be adjusted. I had to adjust the strain reliefs on the big cable so I could unplug the big cable. The big cable had to be unplugged before the silage unloading device could be moved. A powered cable winch system was controlled from the ground, and that was what my neighbor was waiting to power up.

I had just moved the cable and was about three doors down from the top when the neighbor started moving the unloading device. The five-pound plug snapped off the end of the cable and flew right into the four-foot triangle opening in the top of the silo chute. It struck me on the top of my head. It felt like a bolt of electricity shooting through my body. Bright light seemed to fill the chute. I went into a blackout stage as I felt myself slip off the ladder rungs. I felt myself falling but had no control whatsoever. Air seemed to rush by. I couldn't even think. I was totally helpless and a product of gravity. Gravity has no sympathy.

But be not thou far from me, O Lord: O my strength, haste thee to help me. (Psalm 22:19)

Ye that fear the Lord, trust in the Lord: he *is* their help and their shield. (Psalm 115:11)

Let us therefore come boldly unto the throne of grace, that we may obtain mercy, and find grace to help in time of need. (Hebrews 4:16)

For if our heart condemn us, God is greater than our heart, and knoweth all things. (1 John 3:20)

Bang. My head and upper back hit the backside of the chute. It threw me forward, and my feet and legs seemed to slide into something. It felt like I landed on a pillow. I felt like I was caught. My fall had stopped. Everything was happening so fast. I weakly grabbed at the ladder rung and pulled myself toward the silo. I just held on to get my orientation. I felt someone pushing up on me with a shoulder. I was being talked to, but my ears were ringing. I didn't seem to understand what was being said. I was trying to say "thank you," but I wasn't sure if I was even speaking. All of a sudden, my legs seemed to be free. They were in a ladder rung, and I was moving down the ladder. In a short time, I was sitting at the base of the silo.

"Are you okay? Are you *okay?*" my neighbor gasped.

"I will be okay in a minute," I replied.

I was still trying to get my orientation. I seemed to be feeling better in a hurry.

"I saw the big plug hit the ground and stopped lowering the thrower immediately," exclaimed the neighbor. "I looked up the chute and saw you fall. All I could say is, 'God have mercy! God have mercy!' I saw you get caught about halfway or so. I ran up the ladder as fast as I could. That's a lot for an old man. I pushed up on you so that you couldn't fall anymore. I don't know how I got you pushed up enough so I could help you down. Your legs were all the way into the ladder rung—both of them. I don't even know how your boots would fit in there. I had to turn your feet sideways to get them out."

Who hath saved us, and called *us* with an holy calling, not according to our works, but according to his own purpose and grace, which was given us in Christ Jesus before the world began. (2 Timothy 1:9)

Not by works of righteousness which we have done, but according to his mercy he saved us, by the washing of regeneration, and renewing of the Holy Ghost. (Titus 3:5)

145

"Are you okay?" the neighbor asked again.

"I feel just fine," I replied in good spirits.

"Your head is okay? How about your legs? Your neck?" the neighbor asked in back-to-back questions.

I could feel my neighbor trembling as he put his hands on my shoulders. "I'm okay, I replied again as I stood up and started moving around."

"You fell forty feet or so," my neighbor estimated. "All I could say is 'God, have mercy' and 'God, please catch Freddy.' I was just terrified seeing you fall. If you would have fallen all the way, it would have been bad." My neighbor fell to his knees and began to cry. "God, thank you! Father, thank you! Thank you for protecting Freddy."

I put my hand on his shoulder. My neighbor wept and trembled. I felt for him dearly.

"Thank you, Jesus! You have saved me from great harm. You have guarded me many times. May the glory be yours forever! Amen." I kneeled down beside my neighbor. "It's a good day, my friend," I assured him. "It's all good. I feel just fine. We will get this job done and give God the glory for every minute it takes us."

"I have gone to church for many years but never knew how real God was until today," confessed my neighbor. "It's like God is out there somewhere, but you don't really feel him. I have never not believed, but I feel like a new man. You told me once when we went dirt bike riding the Holy Spirit is with us to comfort and protect us. Today I understand! I never could get it in my head that the spirit of God was really with us—I mean right here, right now. I do believe today."

"We do not know how long we will be upon this earth," I offered. "I am not very old, but God has done so much for me. God is in us when we choose to accept Jesus as our savior. The Holy Spirit is with us minute by minute. Life really is how much love of God we can get into ourselves. Sometimes the Spirit is very quiet and sometimes very dynamic. We then give this love in many ways to others."

"I am sixty years old, and I can't remember crying," my neighbor confessed. "I feel so different." He gave me a big hug.

We praised God the entire time we worked to finish the job. We greeted each other with a hug or handshake after that day.

And I will pray the Father, and he shall give you another Comforter, that he may abide with you forever. (John 14:16)

But the Comforter, *which is* the Holy Ghost, whom the Father will send in my name, he shall teach you all things, and bring all things to your remembrance, whatsoever I have said unto you. (John 14:26)

But when the Comforter is come, whom I will send unto you from the Father, *even* the Spirit of truth, which proceedeth from the Father, he shall testify of me. (John 15:26)

He that loveth not, knoweth not God; for God is love. (1 John 4:8)

Love in Christ, Fred

When the Holy Spirit Descends

February 2015

Thought: A letter for you with as much love as it can carry. May the Spirit of God direct you in all ways, this I pray! Let's have a testimonial story and see what we can learn about the Holy Spirit. He touches you lightly in love or aggressively in love.

To all with love,

The mysteries of the universe are held by the Great I Am.

Moses asked our God when he was in the process of doing our Father's request to lead the children of Israel out of Egypt, "Who shall I say has sent me? What is thy name?"

The answer was to say, "I am that I am. Say I am has sent me."

That's a lot to think about in one small bit. When Jesus left this world, he said, "I shall send the Holy Spirit as a comforter to be with you." It's already over my head. So imagine this—if you truly feel the love of our Father, how much more you would draw closer to God and surely be strengthened to hold onto everything he has to offer? I can truly say that the Holy Spirit is that comforter and that love.

In the spring of 1972, I was given the opportunity to go to Minneapolis for an evangelistic crusade rally by Dallas Holms and Jimmy Swaggart. I had been attaining a small Assembly of God church in Minnesota. I found it very generous for a young couple to invite me along with them. I was only sixteen and had no money for such things. I had a friend at his church, which was also invited. I was looking forward to this. We were to meet at the church on a Saturday morning. When I arrived, I found out that my friend would not be going. Pressing matters prevented him from going. I suddenly lost a lot of interest, but I wanted to go just in case God had something for me to learn. I also didn't want to disappoint the folks that gave me the invitation. I knew there were costs involved and, again, how generous.

We stopped for breakfast, and they had insisted on paying. Please, please have anything you want. It may be hard to believe, but my parents have never in my life taken me out for breakfast, lunch, or dinner—I mean before I was sixteen or after. This was such a big thing for me I almost cried. A tear slipped from my eye unintended.

Mary saw that and asked, "Are you okay?"

"Oh, I am fine. I just don't understand your generosity," was my reply. "No one has ever bought me breakfast at a restaurant. I have never bought myself breakfast at a restaurant. I have bought myself a hamburger a couple of times at McDonald's. This seems so, so special. I am a little overwhelmed."

"We eat out so often I just have taken it for granted," John offered apologetically. "I am actually proud that we can do this for you. Let's pray! Father, we humbly come before you and ask you to touch upon Fred's life this day. Let thy Spirit comfort and guide him. Let this be a safe and wonderful time for us. Help us to lift you up and give all the glory to you. Bless this special meal as we ask this in Jesus's name, amen."

The conversations were many and varied on the way to our destination in Minneapolis. One topic was if I had ever been baptized. I explained that I had taken a course at the Lutheran church a few months ago and was sprinkled for a baptism. They in turn explained how the Assembly of God church likes to follow the Bible as close as possible and they do a submersion baptism. I explained how I had been going to the Lutheran church for the last five years. I worked part-time for a farmer, and he picked me up each Sunday for church. I just started driving a few months ago and bought the old pickup they saw me drive up to the church in.

"I saw your sign on the side of your pickup," Mary inserted with a smile. "Did you put 'Jesus Saves' on your pickup?"

"Yes, the day after I bought it," I replied. I have had more people tease me about it rather than compliment me. When I feel God or I am compelled to do something, I just ask him and do it. You see, I have had so many things happen to me already in my life that I would just be ashamed if I walked away from the closeness I have felt. Oh, I had a couple of bullies at school beat me up a few times. I asked God to protect me from them, and that is how I met Roger. You know him. He's a big guy."

"We love Roger. He has a good heart," John reflected. "He has been a part of this church since he was little. He is bigger than most adults. Six foot two, I think. Maybe 240, I guess."

"Well, I was cutting through the gym to avoid these two characters, but they saw me and caught me at the other door. 'Why are you always picking on me?' I asked. 'Because you are a Jesus freak,' Tom snarled with a whiny-creature voice. 'Don't you guys believe in God?' I asked as the medicine ball hit me and knocked the air out of me. They continued throwing a medicine ball at me and wouldn't let me go.

"Roger came running and threw each of them against the wall and then took the medicine ball and threw it at them. He promised them he would find them and finish it if they ever bothered me again. I surely thanked Roger for his help. I told him I thank God for sending him to help me. I had a big red mark on my face from those two. When I went into history class, my teacher, Mr. K., asked me why I had the red mark. I told him about Bill and Tom. I explained what had happened."

"A few days later, they grabbed me after I had left history class," I continued. They were trying to take me into the washroom and dunk me on the stool. All of a sudden, the door slammed open, and there was Mr. K. He grabbed one in each hand and went flying out the door of the restroom with the two and just flung each one into the lockers. He yelled at them about as loud as one could yell.

"Mr. K. is a big guy, and he spent a lot of time in the Marine corps. He demands discipline. He grabbed the two and ran as fast as he could with them to the office. He was yelling that he would just see if there was some way to get them thrown out of school. The next day he made them apologize to me, and each one had to apologize for no less than two minutes. I tell you, it's a long time to just listen to an apology, let alone say it. They have never bothered me since. God did help me, so you see how I love him so."

"Thank you for sharing," Mary spoke excitedly. That is a real testimony to me. It is a real modern-day persecution for standing up for your belief in Jesus Christ. I hope you keep your sign on your pickup for as long as you own it. I don't know if I could stand up for Christ and be persecuted the way the first Christians were persecuted," Mary confessed.

We soon arrive at our destination. We had a few classes before the main speaking event and music. They found a class I should be a part of, and they were going to another. After the event was over, we would meet at the entrance door.

John asked, "Is everything good?"

"Sure, I am fine," I responded.

So we departed. To have told them I felt like I was in a tide pool of people and I felt like I was drowning would have just felt wrong to say, I thought. I tried to listen as best as I could, but my head was numb. These were all good people, but they were still strangers to me.

The class lasted about an hour, and then we left to find seats in the auditorium. I walked out and just stood by the wall and watched people sit here and there. The front thirty rows were just about full, and I was thinking about sitting way in the back. I never saw John or Mary.

I heard a voice. "Hello, my name is Rachael. Hello."

"Oh, sorry," I responded. "I was just thinking about where to sit."

"It must be a hard decision. You have been standing here for a while," Rachael teased.

"I just feel a little out of place here," I answered.

"Here, come with me," Rachael pleaded as she gave me a tug on the arm. "Keep me company so I have someone to sit with."

The name *Rachael* made my ears prick a bit as I had only known the name *Rachael* from one other source—Grandma Hanna's five-year-old Rachael, and she was not with us anymore.

We were soon sitting thirty rows back, and I was listening to her every word. She lived in Minneapolis all her life. She loved going to the A of G she called the church. The church had thousands of members, so this crowd of maybe twenty thousand was no big deal.

"I am sure you will feel the Spirit of God move in this service," Rachael suggested with a smile of excitement.

"What do you mean by move?" I asked.

"Oh, the Holy Spirit will descend on those who believe. He will fill them with love and glorious praises to the Lord. They may even speak in tongues. Lives will be opened and changed forever. Some will come to know Jesus as their savior for the first time," Rachael clamored on excitedly.

"You sure know a lot for only being twelve," I answered surprisingly. "Have you spoken in the tongues, of which you speak?" I asked.

"Many times," Rachael professed. "The first time is when I was eight. I accepted Jesus as my savior when I was eight. I spoke in tongues about a week later. Speaking in tongues is usually an edification of God. I go around praising God all the time. Sometimes people tease me and think I am loopy. I just love my Lord and hope I always will."

"Thank you for being so nice to me," I replied with appreciation. "I feel really comfortable here. I had felt like a fish out of water a little while ago. I prayed that God would give me peace and allow me to be here for him. I think you are an answer to a prayer. Thanks again," I reiterated.

"My parents always say I am an answer to a prayer," Rachael bubbled. "God moves through people, so you need to listen very carefully sometimes to him."

I found the service just wonderful—so many people that were so committed as they reflected testimonies of struggle and triumph. There were stories of healing, which I had never heard of before.

Dallas Holm was a musician committed to Christ. *Great music indeed*, I thought.

The service was coming to an end with an altar call for anyone who wanted to give their life over to Christ, perhaps even to recommit their lives. I thought I would just stay where I was until most of the people left. All of a sudden, I felt myself being pulled to the front of the stage. It is hard to explain. I was going through the rows and not down a row. I didn't seem to be bothering or bumping into anyone. I was soon in front of the stage with my arms extended toward heaven in praise to God. Words unknown to me were just rolling off my tongue like I had spoken them all my life. You feel a love of great comfort like I had never experienced. I have always wanted God to hold me, and I think he was doing just that. I didn't even know that Rachael was standing beside me praising God until I stopped and looked around to see that most people were gone. There were two ministers standing by me with their hands on my shoulders. I didn't even know they were there. *What is this*, I wondered.

John and Mary were just walking to the entrance door.

"I see the party I came with, Rachael, so I best not keep them waiting," I spoke. "I feel so close to God. I wish this feeling would never end."

"This was great," Rachael bubbled with excitement. "This was so wonderful it gives me goosebumps. It was all praise and for such a nice long time. Sometimes there are messages and interpretations."

"You are such a nice person, Rachael. It would be fun to see you again. You are a stranger to no one, Rachael. Thank you for the best day ever."

I wasn't a hugging person, but Rachael didn't have a problem hugging at all.

"May Jesus always move in your life as he does in mine!" Rachael shouted as I left.

I waved and answered with, "Thank you!

John spoke up when I reached them. "Praise God in all his glory for sending his Holy Spirit. It uplifts everyone around and builds your spirit to see or be a part of such an experience. I could sit all day and just bask in this worship. I had one arm around my shoulder from the left and one from the right. It felt like a family.

> And these signs shall follow them that believe; in my name shall they cast out devils; they shall speak with new tongues. (Mark 16:17)

> And there appeared unto them cloven tongues like as of fire, and it sat upon each of them. (Acts 2:3)

> And they were all filled with the Holy Ghost, and began to speak with other tongues, as the Spirit gave them utterance. (Acts 2:4)

> Cretes and Arabians, we do hear them speak in our tongues the wonderful works of God. (Acts 2:11)

> For they heard them speak with tongues, and magnify God. Then answered Peter. (Acts 10:46)

> And when Paul had laid *his* hands upon them, the Holy Ghost came on them; and they spake with tongues and prophesied. (Acts 19:6)

Love in Christ, Fred

Is It a Potato?

March 2015

Thought: A letter for you with as much love as it can carry. May the Spirit of God direct you in all ways, this I pray! Let's have a testimonial story and see what we can learn about continuous protection from our Father in heaven. Miracles we can't explain?

To all with love,

Being twelve years old was a big deal to me. The thought of moving out of childhood appealed to me. It was like moving forward into the final stage to be an adult. I have heard many say, "Don't rush being young. Enjoy it."

I didn't enjoy my childhood and wanted to be an adult, to make my own decisions. When I was even eight or nine, I thought I could make my own decisions. Christ came into my life at eight years old with a family or relatives, which would have no part of it. I was trying to be too independent. Perhaps! One man by the name of Pastor Petersen said he would help me find as much of God as he could. He drove a thirty-mile round trip every Sunday and church event to pick me up. "With God, all things are possible," he always told me.

> Jesus said unto him, "If thou canst believe,
> all things *are* possible to him that believeth."
> (Mark 9:23)

It was the last day of school with a long Christmas vacation ahead. Even this was not a regular day. It was aiming to be a lot of days working in the woods and harvesting trees. It would be work, but I loved the trees. This was better than milking the cows, better than cleaning the pig pens, and better than feeding the sheep. The big trees wouldn't let you put your arms around them: the height that kept them from falling fast as they captured air on the way down, but when they found the ground, they threw up a huge cloud of snow; the rush of breaking branches that warned of standing clear. The word of caution was given to be clear of the area even before the cutting of several big trees. Cut a few trees in one spot, and move to another. This was done for the safety of all concerned. There were a lot of risks in this job: chainsaws slip with an ax, chains breaking, trees twisting and falling wrong, tripping over branches, logs rolling onto a foot or leg, and many more things you didn't want to learn from experience.

The bus rolled into the yard, and my first observation was the family single vehicle was gone. Dad would have that and still be working in the woods. First thing was to greet Mother and baby brothers. Little brothers would think I was great because I had been gone since 7:00 a.m., and it was now 4:30 p.m. It was an hour's bus ride morning and night. They thought the bus was great; just wait, not so much.

It was out to the woodpile and let the cutting begin. It was easier cutting the wood at twelve than it was at eight, plus there were no livestock chores at this time. Dad was laid off from construction in the winter, so it was tree-cutting season. He would be home soon as the darkness crept into the woods by five o'clock. By 5:30 it was dark. The firewood was in for the night. I was cleaned up for supper. The question was where is Dad?

There was a light snow falling, and Mother suddenly said, "Let's eat supper."

We always waited for Dad, but he was delayed.

A few moments later, the silence was broken again when Mother spouted off with, "I hope he didn't get hurt."

I knew Dad wouldn't take any unnecessary risks. "He spent twelve years in the service," I reminded. "Four years fighting in the Pacific, landing two weeks after the bomb was dropped in Japan, and two years fighting from a foxhole in Korea. He is a Marine. He shall return."

We had no phone, and the closest neighbor was four miles away. I felt myself rushing through supper.

"I know where we are working in the woods, Mother," I sounded as I continued to hurry.

It will take me an hour to go and check things out. I will take the flashlight and use it only when I have to. I hurried forward with the meal. The thought of Dad being injured now entered my thoughts. There may have been an accident and Dad was in need of help.

"I will probably meet him on the road on his way home," I added to release the idea of being alarmed. "If I need help, I will go over to Johnson's. That may be another hour."

I walked quickly to the entry, and I started pulling on some warm clothing. I was dressed, but Mother came over and threw a scarf around my neck. I had not a scarf on since I was little. Mother never cried, but I saw a tear in her eye. I gave her a hug.

"I will hurry," I offered. "I am sure everything is fine." I hurried out the door as I felt my face growing warm with emotion.

"Be careful," Mother offered in a broken voice as she closed the door behind me.

The snow continued to fall as I walked down the mile-and-a-half lane. I walked; I trotted, trying to hurry as quickly as possible. I knew accidents happened. It didn't matter if you had been a Marine. I had said what I did to help remove the fear that seemed to be creeping in the home. Darkness loomed as it was clouded over, and the snow fell. I was glad it wasn't cold. I was actually warm as I found myself running. Thoughts started to run through my head. What if Dad was hurt? What if a tree had fallen on him?

I deliberately threw myself into a big snowbank on the side of the road.

"Father in heaven, let my dad be okay," I pleaded as I sucked in oxygen.

I hit the snow with my fist.

"Father, I know I am the only one that goes to your church. Father, I have learned that it is your Holy Spirit that is sent to comfort us. Let it be so. I implore you, precious Spirit of God, to help me with this task. To you is the glory. Amen."

Hurriedly I went on to the end of the lane and the additional half mile. I saw no vehicle. It was usually parked beside the road so as not to get stuck in the lane. I went up the path into a small building site, which led into the woods. I flipped the flashlight on, but the little beam didn't do much. It was quiet, the snow was picking up, and the huge trees loomed skyward. I walked up the short lane to where there was a little red barn. The tractor we used to pull logs out of the woods was sitting by the barn. I touched the engine, but it was cold. Logs had been hauled into town a day or two ago. I walked around the dooryard and scanned the light around. I saw no new log pile. All was quiet. I shouted out and again and again. The single word *Dad* hit the blackness of the woods and was swallowed up. I walked into the woods, scanning the dark. Walking along quickly, I found the spot where we had been cutting. There seemed to be no new wood chips, no logs or trees lying on the ground.

I sounded out the single name *Dad*. I shouted again and again. I listened intently. There was nothing. I quietly said, "Dad. Dad, where are you? Where are you?"

I walked farther into the woods, scanning the small light and peering everywhere.

> Father in heaven, I know you are right here.
> I am so glad I know you. I wish my family did.
> Father, I read a small bit in Genesis last week
> where you were grieved in your heart that you
> had created mankind. I am so sorry about that.
> I hurt in my heart right now. I can only imagine
> how you may have felt. I want to be a loving child
> of yours. I want to talk with you always and walk
> the path you want me to walk on. Pastor Petersen
> said there will be things which will knock me
> over and send me down paths I can't see. I will

feel brokenhearted, but if I call upon you, you will deliver me. Let it be so. Please let it be so.

Be sober, be vigilant; because your adversary the devil, as a roaring lion, walketh about, and seeking whom he may devour. (1 Peter 5:8)

And it repented the LORD that he had made man on the earth, and it grieved him at his heart. (Genesis 6:6)

I followed my tracks back out of the woods and soon found the little red barn.

"Hello, little barn," I whispered.

I don't know why I said that. I was perplexed. I didn't know what to think. I walked back to the road. I searched for tracks where a vehicle may have been parked. I couldn't see anything, but then snow had been falling for some time. I knew I had to hurry home.

The trees and the brush indicated a path into the blackness of the night. The whiteness of the snow seemed to run black. I couldn't really see. I just ran between the trees toward a direction.

"Is this life, Father?" I whispered. All this blackness could run me right into a hole. I prefer the light. I simply trusted the path as I ran on into the blackness.

Every once in a while, I thought I saw a small light. I knew I was getting close to home. Yes, there it was. I was exhausted, but I ran on. Soon I reached the door and quickly opened it. I stood in the open door and stared at Mother standing ten feet away.

I was breathing heavily as I said, "No sign. Nothing."

She stood there. She said nothing. I shut the door and began to undress. I walked over and kissed my mother on the cheek. I gave her a little hug, but her arms hung lifeless. There was no return of the emotion.

I got a drink of water and sat by the table. The house was quiet. My little brothers had gone to bed. I explained to Mother how I had searched, and I could give her no explanation.

"Did you look in the basement for Dad's chainsaw and gas mixture?" I asked.

"My mind has run all over, so I did go down and look. It wasn't there," she said, perplexed.

"I will go down and take another look," I offered.

The basement was a good size but lit up fairly well. My eyes scanned the floor to where the saw usually sat. I walked around, looking the open floor area over. There was nothing, but then I didn't expect to see the saw. I picked and pushed and moved things around. I looked under the potato bin, a large eight-foot-square slatted, raised bin with only a few potatoes left. Maybe twenty potatoes left. We usually had some all the way into spring. The garden wasn't very good this year.

I looked at the canning shelves beside the bin. There were pickles and beets, maybe eighty jars. There were tomatoes, maybe another one hundred jars. I walked around behind the woodstove. The woodpile took up a third of the wall. I had just filled the empty spot. We had to fill it up daily. The pile would only last about three or four days. It would be a big job to fill it then. We had a fuel oil heater but used it sparingly for emergency. I walked over to another wall where a paint cloth hung down from a makeshift shelf. I kicked at the cloth with my hands on my hips. I didn't know where else to look. I couldn't figure out what was going on. My foot struck something unexpectedly. It moved, and the tip of a chainsaw blade tipped out from under the cloth. I kneeled down and lifted up the drop cloth. I pulled out the chainsaw and the can of gas mixture. What did this mean? Dad had not gone to the woods to cut trees. Where was he?

I returned upstairs, leaving the lights on. I walked from the hallway into the kitchen. I stood there for a moment as Mother sat at the table. I stood there thinking for just a moment. She heard me walk in, and when I stopped and didn't say anything, she turned and looked at me.

"It's down there," I said very quietly.

"The chainsaw is downstairs?" she asked.

"Yes, it's there. I had to look quite deliberately," I responded. "It was not where it usually is. It seemed to be hidden under that old drop cloth that hangs from that made-up shelf we sit boxes of important things."

"Show me," Mother insisted.

I stepped aside and let Mother go down first.

When we reached the basement, I saw her look around. I followed her around to the opposite wall until she stopped and stared at the saw on the floor. I walked past her and kneeled down by the saw.

"It was under this cloth, like this," I instructed as I pushed it under and then pulled it back out. She stared at the saw for a while and said nothing.

After what seemed like an eternity, I said, "Where?"

There was no response as Mother turned and went upstairs. I followed her back to the kitchen.

She just said, "Go to bed."

I replied, "Good night," but it was the first time I didn't see any good about it.

As I opened the door to go upstairs, a blast of cold hit me. It made you hurry to get into bed. On a very cold day, you could freeze water up here, but the big feather comforters would keep you toasty. Dad had always been home. It felt strange. Mother had known what it was like to have Dad gone for long, long periods of time. I thought it would be a restless night, but I was out and only awakened to a breaking light coming in the window near the bed.

As I went downstairs, breakfast appealed to me, and then I would just spend most of the day cutting firewood. No one was up, and it was seven o'clock. Milk, no. There was no cereal. Toast, no. There were only a couple of slices of bread. I would save them for someone else. I looked outside, and it was snowing hard. It looked like it had been snowing most of the night. I went to the sink to get a drink. In the process, I saw a potato on the counter and picked it up. We often had eggs and fried potatoes for breakfast. I walked to the refrigerator to have a look for eggs. No eggs! It was nice when we had chickens. No more livestock, sad. I still had the potato in my hand, so I walked to the sink and gave it a wash. I had never eaten a potato that wasn't cooked in some way. I started eating it, and it wasn't too bad. I started getting dressed while I ate the potato.

> Thou shalt call, and I will answer thee: thou
> wilt have a desire to the work of thine hands. (Job
> 14:15)

Finally outside, it was like stepping into a different world. There seemed like a foot of snow on the ground, and it was snowing hard. I removed the shovel from the side of the house and cleared the stoop and walkway. There was usually a vehicle at the end of the walk. I started clearing the spot where it would sit, but after a few shovels, I stopped.

"Why bother?" I whispered.

I went to the back door, which led to the basement, and shoveled a path to the woodpile and cleaned an area by the pile. The pile had a lot of snow on it. We were to cut the wood with the bucksaw and not the chainsaw. The chainsaw cost more and was more expensive to run and maintain. I would use the chainsaw. I went to the basement and made ready the saw. There was no gas mixture for the chainsaw. It was the bucksaw again. I used the sled to get the wood to the house and dumped it into the basement stairway. I was excited at the moment because of the amount of wood I was accumulating in the basement. I would fill the basement with as much as I could get down there.

Mother popped her head out of the basement doorway. "Come in and eat something," she suggested.

I dumped my wood down the stairs and went to wash up. I walked to the kitchen and picked up on the smell of fresh bread. *Ah, heavenly*, I thought.

"Do you have ingredients for making bread?" I asked with a bit of optimism.

"We did, and now we don't," Mother replied. "I had enough for two small loaves. There were dill pickles, beet pickles, cooked carrots, and baked potatoes."

"We have carrots?" I asked.

"We had some, and now we don't," Mother added.

"I'm going back to the woodpile."

"You have enough," Mother chimed in.

"I wished I had done this before," I replied. "I am going to pile the basement full. I'm sad and so I will just keep busy. Pastor Petersen will not be out tomorrow to get me for church."

With that, I left and went back to work. The basement was getting full. I had never seen it this full. We were to never stack wood too close to the wood burner. I thought I would stay back about five feet. I came close to the potato bin with my piling. It caught my attention. Yesterday there were about twenty potatoes, but today there were fifteen.

> Six days shall work be done: but the seventh
> day *is* the Sabbath of rest, a holy convocation; ye
> shall do no work *therein*: it *is* the Sabbath of the
> Lord in all your dwellings. (Leviticus 23:3)

I fell to my knees. "Father, we need more potatoes," I whispered. "Let it be so. I walked into the night once to seek you, and once I walked into a snowstorm to talk to you, but this time I am going to stay on my knees."

I stayed for a good while until I moved slightly to one side and felt something bump my knee. Upon looking, I saw a potato by my knee. I picked it up and rubbed it, squeezed it, and realized it was a potato. It hit me with emotion. I took a large breath and sat back. As I sat back, I opened my eyes and saw another potato by my knee. I picked it up and looked at it. It was good, and it made me smile. I looked under the edge of the potato bin and picked up some more. I looked at each one, and they all were good. Now I had a total of forty potatoes.

The first thought to cross my mind was that they had just fallen out of the bin. I laid them on the slats in the bin altogether. They didn't fall through.

"Thank you, Father," I whispered. "Thank you! I don't know how these potatoes got here. I can't make a potato, but I need them to live. Thank you for your mercy."

I took a deep breath so the tears wouldn't come. I was a bit perplexed but very happy. I just didn't care how those potatoes got there; I was ever so grateful. I know there is a God who can do all things; I just don't know how.

But God, who is rich in mercy, for his great
love wherewith he loved us. (Ephesians 2:4)

The next day I continued to cut and stack wood by the back door until dark. The wind was coming up; the temperature was dropping. I could see the snow blowing over the woodpile. *Oh boy*, I thought. All of this snow and wind, the woodpile would get buried, and I couldn't stop it. I thought about continuing when Mother stuck her head out the basement door. It startled me as I was standing beside the door.

"Come in and let tomorrow take care of itself," she ordered. "Let's have supper."

I went in and washed up for supper.

When I entered the kitchen, Mother asked, "Where did the other potatoes come from?"

I remembered what she had told me at lunchtime. We had some, but now we have none. "We had some, and now we have more," I quipped and smiled. I couldn't help myself.

"What?" she asked.

"I prayed, and a potato appeared—and then another and another until there were forty potatoes," I explained.

"Stop it," she demanded.

"Really, along the edge of the potato bin on the floor," I insisted.

"Never mind, I was being serious," she snapped. Mother walked over close to me face-to-face and in a quiet and serious tone said, "We don't have much food, we don't have transportation, we don't have money, and we are being snowed in. I don't know how much more I can take."

I said no more but went to the table and sat down.

I bowed my head and said, "Father, thank you for this food we are about to receive. We are truly grateful. Amen."

We had bread, pickles, and potatoes. If we had a cow, we would have milk. I wish we had kept one cow and a couple of dozen chickens. We did have life, and we were not sick. I wasn't to bring my prayer to the table, but today I just did.

The wind just ripped and howled all night and the next day and the next. When would it stop?

"Go to the basement and get the rest of the potatoes?" Mother asked.

"Yes," I responded.

For some reason, it gave me a chill as I went to the basement. I stood by the potato bin and counted the potatoes. There were fifteen potatoes. That was the amount I had first seen before more seemed to appear. It made me fall to my knees. I felt like a blast of wind pushed me down, but there was no wind. Maybe my knees were weak. Maybe I was afraid, but I didn't feel afraid.

"Father, we need more potatoes," I whispered. "Let it be so."

I felt something hit me with emotion. I took a large breath and sat back. As I sat back, I opened my eyes and saw a potato by my knee. I picked it up and looked at it. It felt like it was three days ago. I looked under the bin and found another and another. I crawled under the bin and gathered all I could see. It was good, and it made me smile. I looked under the edge of the potato bin and picked up some more. I looked at each one, and they all were good. Now I had a total of fifty potatoes. I laid them on the slats in the bin altogether. They didn't fall through.

"Thank you, Father," I whispered. "Thank you! Thank you for your mercy."

I took a deep breath so the tears wouldn't come. Why fifteen, why forty, and now we had fifty. After I had them all lined up in the bin and toughly counted, I shouted out, "May I never forget your love, Father."

I can't explain the potatoes, but who cares when you have a God that loves you?

Mother shouted down the stairs, "Are you okay?"

"Yes, but I need some help. Come down and see," I requested.

Soon Mother was standing beside me. She stared at the potatoes. I just smiled.

She looked at me and asked, "Why are you smiling?"

"We have some, and now we have more," I joked.

"Stop saying that," she spoke very sweetly.

I gave her a hug just because. "I fell to my knees. I asked God for potatoes like before. I found one by my knee, and I looked under the bin and found more," I spoke quickly and gave an explanation.

"Is there more under there?" Mother asked.

"I got all of them I could see," I said with a shrug.

Mother bent over and had a look but said nothing. I felt an onion in the hanging bag the other day.

"Let's make potato soup," I implored.

We took the onion sac down and emptied it out. There were five onions.

"Let's leave one and take four," I suggested.

"Stop it! It makes no sense," Mother insisted.

We took potatoes and onions and went to make some supper. We would use all of the potatoes, including the skins. We used to peel them, but that sounded wasteful.

It was three days before the wind subsided. We just stayed in the house and watched the snow pile up. I was so glad I had brought in weeks of firewood. Mother gave me a rare "I am proud of you." I had a little rice in some tomato soup mixture for breakfast. This would be the breakfast meal for a while. I would go out and clear some snow. I had gone out every so often to clear the snow away from the door so the door could be opened. We thought the snowplow would come in a few days to clear the road.

I shoveled snow for a while with a reluctant brother. He became too much of a fuss, so I told him we would take a break and explore the driveway to see how much snow was in it. I yelled into the house to let Mother know what we were up. She just responded with a "Fine," so we're off.

The drifts were up to the eve of the barns. We were excited to see such a massive amount of snow. I saw the door on the machine shed where the tractor was parked inside. The snow was at least ten feet deep for about twenty feet, and then it tapered down to about three feet. We stood there looking at the snow.

"Well, brother, that's your job," I instructed. "You have to dig the tractor out so we can use it to push snow."

"I couldn't throw it out. I would have to find something to haul it with. I couldn't move that much snow in a lifetime," he complained.

"That may be true," I responded as I put my arm around his shoulder. We just stood there for a minute and stared at the mountain of snow.

"Let's go explore the driveway," I suggested.

"Okay," he responded, excited.

We took off running. The snow was very hard after being so cold and pounded by the wind. The drifts started out at maybe three then four then five feet tall. They quickly grew into small cliffs. We were standing on the top of deep snow and struggled to climb seven and eight feet straight up to the top of some drifts. It started out as just fun, but soon it became a real challenge to climb some of the drifts. We sat down on the top of a huge drift. We just stared in disbelief.

"I have never seen anything like this," I told my brother.

"Me either, but boy, is this fun," he replied excitedly.

"Yeah, maybe, but do you think the snowplow can get through this?" I asked.

"Well, I don't know," he said seriously. "What if it can't?" he asked.

"That's a good question," I offered, feeling perplexed. "Maybe they have bigger machines for this deep snow."

We went maybe a third of the way down the driveway, finding one cliff after another. We decided that it was such a challenge, so we had better start back.

"We have a lot of snow to move just to get at the woodpile," I instructed my brother.

"Ah, don't say that," he responded in his whiney voice. "I will hate snow if I have to scoop it all day."

"Not just all day but all day and all night," I suggested.

We finally returned to the house, and as soon as we got in the door, we just fell on the floor. We were panting as if we had run a mile.

"Well, what? What did you see?" Mother asked as we lay on the floor.

"We saw snow and more snow," I laughed.

My brother chimed in, "There are cliffs as high as the barn. It's like climbing a mountain. The snow is taller than our woodpile. Boy, is it fun! I want to go down the road some more before the snowplow pushes it away."

We just lay there as my brother rambled on. "Mother, how does a snow plow push snow that is higher than the snowplow?" my brother asked.

"Don't ask such silly questions," she responded. "Just wait and see how they do it when they get here."

"When will the snowplow get here?" he asked.

"I don't know?" she sternly replied.

"Let's go back out and start moving snow from the woodpile," I instructed.

We both reluctantly went out to the woodpile and stared at it. You could only see a piece or two that indicated where the pile was located.

"If the snow had covered those two ends, we wouldn't know where the pile of firewood was at." My brother disclaimed the very thoughts I was having. "How do we start?" he asked.

"Well, there is less snow over the top of the pile, but then we would have to pull all the big pieces out to cut them. If we dig a path to the pile and open up the front of the pile, we will be digging snow for days and days," I replied as I was trying to think of something. "We have maybe five days, I think."

"I am glad you got so much wood in a few days ago," my brother offered in appreciation. He placed one arm around me in a half hug. I returned the gesture with an arm on his shoulder.

"Let's do the least amount of work," I suggested. "We will dig the snow off the top and throw it to the northwest. It will help from filling what we have dug out from blowing back in. The snow shovels didn't seem to work very well. The snow was very hard."

"Now what?" asked my little brother.

"Well," I muttered. "We need a sharper shovel or something to cut the snow out. The sand shovels and spades are in the machine shed with the tractor. Let's go see if there is a way into the shed. Maybe we can get in the window on the back of the shed."

We were off to the shed. It looked like another five feet of drifting, and you could have buried the machine shed. When we got to the back of the machine shed, the drift was all the way up onto the roof, and it was the whole forty-foot length of the shed. We walked to the southeast corner, and we could see a space between the wall and the big drift. The space was two to three feet wide. It was like a tunnel. With a little digging, we could get into the space. The snow in the bottom of the tunnel was almost up to the bottom of the windows. We started to crawl down into the tunnel.

My little brother responded with, "Spooky, but this is fun."

"Maybe, but go slow," I suggested.

We made our way to the first window and tried to open it. It wouldn't budge. It was onto the second window, but we had the same result. Onto the third and last window, but it was no good.

"Well, the tools are hanging on that end of the shed where the first window is at."

We made our way back to the first window and tried it again. No good!

"We will have to break the window," I suggested.

"I'm not going to break it," my brother confessed. "Dad would be mad."

"Where is Dad?" I answered.

"I don't know! I will tell him I broke the window when he comes back." With that, I jabbed the handle of the snow shovel through the lower part of the two sash windows. Glass flew in, and I continued to break the glass around the edge. This was done to prevent from getting cut when we crawled in.

"I will go in and hand some stuff to you, brother." I crawled in on the workbench and dropped onto the floor. I quickly found a sand shovel and handed it out through the window. "Try to toss the shovel up and out through the hole in the snow we made," I suggested.

I went back to look for another sharp shovel. I found a square short-handle shovel. *This is great*, I thought. I grabbed it and shoved it out the window.

"Here's a good one," I said excitedly.

"How about a snow-cutting saw?" my little brother suggested.

"Snow cutting, snow cutting," I muttered.

There was a very long hand saw with big teeth. I think it was called a bucksaw.

"How about this one?" I spouted, and with that, I shoved it out the window.

"This thing looks wicked," my little brother said with surprise. "I bet it could cut ice."

I hauled it to the bench and climbed back upon the bench. We ended up digging steps into the snow to get the job done. We hauled our confiscated goods up to the basement.

"Now what is next?" my brother asked.

"Get your sled from beside the house, and I am going to take the saw and see what happens when I cut a snow block," I instructed.

The snow was about three feet deep then five feet deep and then about ten feet deep to the woodpile. We went up to the five-foot level and cut into the snowbank with the saw. We cut a two-foot square block, took the square-faced shovel, and pried it out and onto the sled. The sled moved the block with ease, so we pulled it a short way and dumped it off.

"This is kind of fun," said my little brother. "Let's keep going and see how we do," I encouraged.

The snow was just the right hardness. We cut two blocks wide and two blocks deep. The front of the woodpile was found in about twelve feet. You would have thought we found gold with all the celebration and carrying on. We cut another double row of blocks and hit the face of the woodpile again. We were terrific and celebrated again.

"Cut two more blocks wide on the other side," suggested my little brother.

We cut the blocks from the other side, shoveled some snow, and the next thing we could see was the top half of the woodpile. It was getting dark as we shoveled the last bit of snow off the top of the wood we had exposed. At that moment, Mother called for supper. We grabbed our tools and went to the basement with them.

"Tomorrow we cut wood," I proclaimed.

"Tomorrow we cut," exclaimed my brother.

The next morning, we were up and eating our tomato and rice soup.

"I am getting tired of this soup," whined my brother.

"Never complain about what you do have," I voiced sternly. "Would you rather have no soup?"

> Loves not sleep, lest thou come to poverty; open thine eyes, *and* thou shalt be satisfied with bread. (Proverbs 20:13)

> He that loveth silver shall not be satisfied with silver; nor he that loveth abundance with increase: this *is* also vanity. (Ecclesiastes 5:10)

We went to cutting with the bucksaw. It was right on top of the pile, and we went on cutting until there were too many pieces to cut and they were in the way. My brother kept hauling on his sled, dumping them into the basement way; and every once in a while, we would go to the basement and stack. It was going very nicely, and by dark, we had the base fuller than before. Mother called for supper, so we shut it down.

We patted each other on the back as we went into the kitchen. We were a team; we were the best of brothers. We were the best of each other.

"What's that chocolate smell?" asked my little brother.

"They are cupcakes," replied Mother.

"Cupcakes!" we said with surprise. "Where did they come from?" we again added excitedly.

"I made them for our Christmas," Mother offered. "Today is Christmas. We had forgotten. We had not gone to the woods and gotten a tree. There are no presents, but there are cupcakes," Mother explained.

"We love cupcakes, and we love you," we both chimed.

"You can have as many cupcakes as you want," Mother offered. This was a first. It was usually one.

It was potatoes, beet pickles, dill pickles, tomato juice, cupcakes, and more chocolate cupcakes. What a happy little meal. There were games and cocoa made with water and sugar. We stayed up late playing games until we were just tired of games. I told the Christmas story and what it meant. Mother even asked questions. I was delighted. It was now two weeks of being snowed in with no sign of a snowplow. Tomorrow we would cut wood and pile it by the basement door until we could pile no more.

As I went to sleep, I thanked Christ Jesus for the day and what he had done for this family.

> Father, holy Father, please do not grieve that you have created mankind. We thank you for sending your Son that we may have life eternally with you. Forgive me and my family of our sins. Help us to please you and give you the glory for all you do for us, even unto the smallest of things. Thank you for helping Mother to listen to your story and even asking questions. May her prayers be answered if she should have any prayers? It's almost one year since my appendices broke and I came close to dying. Thank you for giving me a little more life! Let it be so. Please let it be so. Amen.

> "And it shall come to pass in that day, I will hear," saith the LORD, "I will hear the heavens, and they shall hear the earth." (Hosea 2:21)

> For the eyes of the Lord *are* over the righ-
> teous, and his ears *are open* unto their prayers:
> but the face of the Lord *is* against them that do
> evil. (1 Peter 3:12)

We went downstairs the next morning; we were excited to get started. We would just keep piling the wood by the back door. The basement was full.

We walked by the potato bin, and my brother whispered, "There are no potatoes."

I looked at the bin and set the saw down. I couldn't breathe for a moment. I felt a tear coming to my eye.

"What will we eat?" my brother asked.

"We...we will eat tomatoes, pickles, and beet pickles," I suggested.

I put my hand on my brother's shoulder and stared at the potato bin. "Father, please bring us food. Show us your mercy in Jesus's name," I prayed. Then we just stood there.

"Will God give us more food?" asked my brother.

"Yes, he will. Believe with all your heart," I whispered to him. "Let's take the potato bin apart; it will be easy," I explained very soberly.

I grabbed a hammer by the door and began to knock the boards apart. "Just stand the boards on end in the corner. Move the empty burlap feed sacks over to the shelving on the other wall. Fold them in half so they stack up and don't fall over."

We continued on, and the bin came apart quickly.

"There is something in this sack," sounded my brother.

I stopped and looked toward him. "What?" I asked as I walked over to him.

He opened the top of the sack and put his head into it. "Potatoes, potatoes," he said with his head inside the sack. He jumped with excitement.

I folded the bag back and looked at the potatoes. "Maybe a hundred!" I shouted. I lifted the bag down. If a bag was full, it would be a hundred pounds.

We threw the rest of the empty burlap bags on the floor. There was another bag beside the first, and when my brother stuck his head into the bag, he sounded, "Carrots, carrots!"

I folded the bag down, and sure enough, I lifted it off the shelf and sat it on the floor. "There must be fifty pounds of carrots!" I shouted.

We danced a jig and shouted, "Carrots, potatoes, carrots, potatoes!"

"What's going on down there?" Mother shouted.

"We found gold!" I shouted back.

We both started to jig again and shouted, "Gold, gold."

In a minute, Mother showed up. We stopped and just watched her intently. She came over and looked into the bags. We kept quiet and watched her.

"Where did they come from?" she asked.

"From heaven," I said. "Remember how we carried the potatoes and carrots in from the garden? We put them in the burlap sacks and carried them in. We dumped the potatoes in the bin and left the carrots in the sacks. We put the bags of carrots in a row on the floor. We must have thought that these two bags were carrots and ended up sitting them on this shelf. We emptied the other sacks and sat them up here on this shelf. We just buried these two sacks with empty ones, or is it a gift from heaven?"

We started jigging again and shouting, "Carrots, potatoes, carrots, potatoes!" We grabbed ahold of Mother's hands so she would join in. She laughed until she cried. She grabbed each of us and kissed us on the forehead.

"From heaven, Mother, from heaven!" I shouted.

She just smiled, but oh so sweet.

When Mother left to go back upstairs, I put the two sacks back on the shelf.

We went back to cutting wood. We cut and piled as close to the house as we could. The wind didn't blow, and the sun did shine.

It was near the end of the week when we heard a sound in the distance. We had a mile-and-a-half driveway with trees lining it all the way. It was a roaring sound like a big engine. We gazed toward the sound. We could see black smoke every once in a while. We ran to the house.

"Mother, Mother!" we shouted. "Come and listen."

We stood on the stoop and watched, listened, watched, and listened. We didn't make a peep.

My brother whispered, "What is it?"

"I think they are clearing our driveway with a caterpillar," Mother replied very slowly.

"Can we go down the driveway and see?" we both shouted.

"No, no!" Mother sternly commanded. "Stay here! You can see when they get in sight."

Mother returned to the house, and we went back to the wood. When we hauled the wood to the pile by the house, we roared like the sound of a big engine. We did that all afternoon, but we could see the black smoke get to be more obvious as it got closer.

The caterpillars got closer and revealed the power of what they were doing. We quickly sat down on the sled, which we strategically placed on top of the snowdrift. There were two of them. They were running at an angle to the driveway and pushing snow, brush, trees, and everything in their way. They pushed everything about forty or fifty feet off the drive. When they hit the bigger trees, the engines would roar extra loud with the black exhaust just rolling out. This was different and exciting. One pushed on one side and the second on the other.

When they were just about to turn in the driveway, one straightened out and followed the path into the yard. It came charging up through the dooryard as if the three to four feet of continuous snow was nothing. It turned and came right toward our woodpile. It came to a sudden stop, and the driver climbed down. The big machine sat there on an idle.

"Hello, boys," the man greeted. "How do you like my cat?"

"We love it," we both sounded out.

"Is your dad here?" the man asked.

"He's lost," I replied.

"Lost?" the man asked.

"My name is Ralph, and the other operator is Bill. Was your dad lost in the snowstorm?"

"No, I don't think so," I replied.

"How long has he been lost?" asked Ralph.

"Since December 18 of last month," I informed Ralph. "He didn't come home from cutting trees. I went looking for him but didn't find him."

"I see. Is there anything I can do for you?" Ralph asked.

"You could push the snow away from this woodpile, away from the machine shed, so we could get the tractor out," I instructed. "Clear the dooryard too."

"We surely can do that," offered Ralph as he went back to the cat.

We moved up to the house to watch some more. The snow in the dooryard disappeared in a few minutes. The big drifts around the woodpile quickly moved out of the way. Ralph pushed the whole woodpile closer to the house. We will be able to cut up most of it and throw it right into the basement. *Sweet*, I thought.

The cats came to a stop and shut down. A pickup showed up about the same time.

"We will come back tomorrow and pick up the cats," Ralph informed us. "Can I talk to your mother for a minute?"

"Yes sir," I replied. I went to the door to get Mother. "Mother, Ralph wants to talk to you," I requested.

"Have Ralph step inside?" Mother asked.

"Sir, Mother wants you to step inside to talk," I requested of Ralph.

My brother and I went over by the other two men and the cats. They showed us stuff and let us climb up on the cats. We continued our involvement until Ralph returned.

"We will see you boys tomorrow when we return to get the cats!" Ralph shouted as he went to the pickup.

We watched them drive away and went to pick up our tools.

There was a sit-down conversation after supper: Don't talk about where Dad is or isn't to anyone. Mother would do the talking. We would probably not be staying on the farm anymore. We would move somewhere, but she didn't know where. My heart was broken. Life should just be over, I thought. Tonight I would talk to God instead of sleeping. Tomorrow was Saturday. I was sure I would see Pastor Petersen on Sunday.

> Sorrow *is* better than laughter: for by the sadness of the countenance the heart is made better. (Ecclesiastes 7:3)

> Peace I leave with you, my peace I give unto you: not as the world giveth, give I unto you. Let not your heart be troubled, neither let it be afraid. (John 14:27)

I whispered:

> My Father, my Father, I have a great sadness. You have been so good to us. You have unhidden the hidden food. You have made food come from I do not know where. We live, and I am grateful. It is by thy hand that I believe all good things come from. Be with me as I believe my path goes in many directions. I know my mother has a great sadness upon her. Help me to do according to your will in my best for her. I do not know where my dad is lost to, but let thy Holy Spirit guard his path. Anyone that has fought in so many battles and has told me that he thought everyday was his last has worn shoes which I could never wear. I cast myself before you. I believe that he shall return. Let it be so! Let it be so! Amen.

I talked with God for a long time until sleep caught me unaware. Mother was making fried potatoes and warm tomato juice when I arrived in the kitchen.

"I had the cat man call your uncle and ask him to come down and visit us today," Mother informed me. "Ralph told me that Jerry, our neighbor who drives the grader, had informed him that he would not be able to open our driveway. The county would have to find some equipment to do the job. I guess it just took over two weeks to get the equipment to get it done. If you see them getting the equipment today, please thank them again."

I had just finished eating when I looked out the window to see Pastor Petersen's black-with-yellow-fin '57 Chevrolet drive up. I ran outside, and a station wagon pulled up also. Pastor and Mrs. Petersen were getting out. My heart leaped with joy at seeing them.

"Good morning, I am so glad to see you, I said excitedly, hugging Mrs. P. I ran around the front and hugged Pastor. I was usually more formal with a handshake, but it just felt like more was needed. I recognized Mr. and Mrs. Anderson from church in the wagon. I ran and hugged them too.

"Good morning, I am so glad to see you," I gasped.

"See what we have for you," they all seem to say at the same time. They opened up the doors and trunks of the vehicles. The cars were so full of just everything.

Pastor P said. "Let's start hauling it in the house." So we did.

It overfilled the kitchen—and we had a big kitchen. It took a good while to get that all done. We visited for a while, but they didn't know that Dad wasn't there—or did they as nothing was said. Nothing was said, but it felt uncomfortable. They only knew that we were stranded for over three weeks.

We were ever so grateful. These were my people, my God-loving, fearing, and worshiping people.

"Thank you, Father in heaven, for people like this," I whispered as they left.

A couple of neighbors came over with a lot of stuff. Two aunt and uncle families came over and brought more and a lot more.

We were asked to go outside and do something while the adults had a conversation. We went out and talked about nothing. We looked at the cats for a while and climbed some snowbanks. Soon we saw the pickup from yesterday that Ralph and Bill left in. It was followed by two large trucks. The two trucks pulled up into the door-yard side by side. Everyone got out, shouting hello and how are you.

I found Ralph and greeted him specially. "Good afternoon, Ralph. I want to thank you for all you have done. It seems...it seems like you really saved us. I am ever so grateful." I felt a little emotional and just hugged him too.

"You are more than welcome. I am sorry it took so long to find operators and equipment."

We stood back and let them load up the equipment. They were done in a half hour and on their way.

After the crew left, my uncles came out and wanted to talk to us.

They said, "I don't think your dad is going to come back. We don't know where he is, but we do know he cashed a logging check a distance away from here. We know some other things, but we can't tell you about those things. Your mother can tell you when she feels right about it."

"I know he is kind of lost right now, but somehow, someway he will come back," I said somberly.

"Why do you say that?" they inquired.

I kicked at the ground and looked straight at my uncles and told them, "I prayed, and I believe that with God all things are possible. I know you all and Mother don't believe, but I have made God part of my life. I have seen God do things for me. Remember my six days in a coma with my appendix, my scarlet fever, bad whooping cough twice, mumps, chickenpox, measles, the wild cat trying to get me, face to face with that big bear, and now I am adding my potatoes to the list of special gifts from God. I am going to pray my dad home."

"We hope you're right, but sometimes you just have to see the way things are," one uncle commented.

> By faith Enoch was translated that he should not see death; and was not found, because God had translated him: for before his translation he had this testimony, that he pleased God. (Hebrews 11:5)

> Jesus answered and said unto them, "Verily
> I say unto you, 'If ye have faith, and doubt not,
> ye shall not only do this which is done to the fig
> tree, but also if ye shall say unto this mountain,
> "Be thou removed, and be thou cast into the sea,"
> it shall be done.'" (Matthew 21:21)

When I go to sleep at night, I pray; I just talk to God. I listen. My sleep pattern has always been poor, but that only means I can talk to God and stay awake. Tonight's prayer would be a test. I have felt protected from many things which could have harmed me. If God wanted me to live, it was his will. If he wanted to take me home to heaven, so be it. I would not knowingly take risks with this body and mind. Pastor Petersen had told me to care for myself, for my body is the temple of the Holy Spirit.

> What? know ye not that your body is the
> temple of the Holy Ghost which is in you, which
> ye have of God, and ye are not your own? (1
> Corinthians 6:19)

> Most Holy Father and my Lord and Savior
> Jesus Christ, you know that I don't always like
> asking for something for me but for the greater
> good of those around me. You have protected
> me from things, which I hadn't even asked to be
> protected from. I do ask, Father, for your protec-
> tion from that which I can see and that which
> I cannot see. I do this because I know you can
> and will. It makes me feel good and helps me feel
> your awesomeness. Lord, you know what I am
> going to ask before I do so. The plan you have is
> greater than I can imagine. I pray for my brothers.
> I pray for my mother. I pray for those who don't
> believe. There is a great sadness, anger, and a feel-
> ing of hopeless life. I know, Father, that prayers

don't need length or repetition or shouting to the masses. Dear Jesus, I pray for the return of my dad. I don't know if he is hurt. I don't know if he is lost. I don't know if he is just too sad about life. I don't know if he is being pulled away. Whatever it is, you know what it is. I know you can forgive all things. I will forgive, and I will love my dad. I believe, Father, that you will bring my dad back to us. I will stand on this. I will not test thee. I will have faith. I will have patience. I may not be able to talk to anyone about this, but I know I can talk to you. I would rather talk to you. In you is my strength. I am only twelve. I know I will fail you many times in my life. I am sorry before I even commit such things. Forgive me of my sins. Let it be so! Let it be so! Amen.

The school bus had gone by the driveway all last week. Today it roared into the yard to pick us up for school. It was a strange welcoming as everyone on the bus roared with excitement, appreciation, jealousy, and thankfulness. It started again when we reached school. I never knew how many people really cared. I thought it seemed like we were all connected in some way. We talked of snow, of storms, and of dangers therein, but I never talked of Dad. I knew we were going to move sometime, yet I could say nothing. I knew that one word was controlled by a thousand. My heart was breaking and would break more. I must find strength. May God give me strength! I knew we would depart, but I didn't know how or when.

The weeks tumbled by. My uncle stopped by once a week to take care of my mother's requests. I was well ahead on firewood, but on Saturdays, I cut firewood. I went into the edge of the woods and cut trees. I would sled the pieces back to the pile by the house. I knew Mother wouldn't want me cutting down trees. "Too dangerous," she would say. I would use the ax and split logs. I would drive out the emotion of the weak. When you aggressively split logs, it will drive everything out of you." I will not be filled with anger; I would speak as I would swing. I will have the faith of ten thousand as the ax would swing. I will put my God before myself. I will fight as ten thousand for him.

January, February, March and then we were into April. April, April, you are sometimes a cruel April. It was the first Thursday of April and the third anniversary of the tragic death of a very dear friend. I arrived home from school, and as I came off the bus, here came Mother walking over to meet us.

"Your dad is home," she said with a smile. "Give him a hug, and let him know you love him."

My little brother bounced into the house like a puppy missing its owner. I opened the door, held it for Mother. I walked to my dad as he sat by the kitchen table.

"I love you, Dad. I always have," I said soberly.

He continued to sit and said nothing.

I put my arm around his shoulder and just stood there for about fifteen minutes. "I give God the glory for your return. May you be well and happy," I offered up with hope.

Dad was kind of staring into space. I looked at Mother, and she shook her head at me side to side or a no-no at me. She didn't want me to say anything.

"Go see if we need a bit of wood carried in," she suggested to me.

I went to the basement, and she followed me.

"Don't preach at your dad, and keep your conversations very short and general?" she asked. "All you need to know is that your dad was in a very bad accident. In time he will be just fine. You don't need to bring in any wood. I want you to go upstairs and pack everything. I have boxes in the living room. Your uncle is coming in with his big truck, and we are going to load everything that will fit. If it doesn't fit, we will not take it. The tractors, equipment, and everything outside will be sold. Your uncle will see to that."

"What about school tomorrow?" I asked in an anxious manner. "Saturday we are going to Southern Minnesota. We have a house there to move into," Mother explained.

"My friends, Pastor Petersen, and the people I know, what about them?" I asked.

"I am sorry," Mother offered with sympathies. "I need your help and nothing else," she added. "I have to go make supper."

It would be like disappearing from the face of the earth, I thought.

Thank you, Father! You answered my prayer. I asked, I believed, and I trusted in you. For some reason I am in awe. I am an emotional bag zipped shut. I feel like I could explode. Mother seems calm and happy. Brothers are as happy as monkeys in a tree. I don't feel any love here. I am going to lose friends en masse. I am, however, in awe that you have delivered my dad. It's three months, but it's all good. I think I am going to have the strangest life ever.

For therein is the righteousness of God revealed from faith to faith: as it is written, the just shall live by faith. (Romans 1:17)

Peace I leave with you, my peace I give unto you: not as the world giveth, give I unto you. Let not your heart be troubled, neither let it be afraid. (John 14:27)

Love in Christ, Fred

God's Mysterious Ways

— ❧ —

April 2015

Thought: A letter for you with as much love as it can carry. May the Spirit of God direct you in all ways, this I pray! Let's look into a testimonial story to show you how paths of each other can cross for a short time and last forever.

To all with love,

A very gracious young lady, by the name of Elaine, came into my life when I was eight. We were partnered together in school to help each other get the best education that we could get. I was very good at math but no good at English. Elaine was very good at English and not so good at math. The whole class of twenty-two students was matched together in this fashion. All of the third-grade year was like this, and surprise, the four grades went the same way. Yes, it was another year together. I had just come to know about Jesus in third grade, and as it happened, Elaine loved to talk about God and his Son, Jesus Christ. I helped Elaine with her school studies, and she filled me Jesus. When you feel good about something, you do well. With Pastor Peterson from the Assembly of God picking me up and traveling some thirty miles each time and Elaine answering all my various questions, it was just great. I didn't have many friends, but those I did have meant the world to me. There were two people I would fight a bear for.

But whoso keepeth his word, in him verily
is the love of god perfected: hereby know we are
in him. (1 John 2:5)

It was early April, and I had arrived on the one-hour bus trip to the school in Menahga, Minnesota. I always watched for my friend Elaine walking to school, for she lived in town. If she was close to the crosswalk, to cross the street to school, I would wait and we would walk into the building together. I don't know if I ever saw her without a smile. She lived with her grandparents and never knew her own parents. It didn't seem to affect her though I felt for her.

On this day it was very foggy, but I saw her ready to cross the street as I stood up on the bus, preparing to get off. I would wait for her and walk into the school. She was with her friend Julie as I observed them starting to walk across the street and waiting for the others to get off the bus, as I was setting near the back of the bus. All of a sudden, a car passed the bus, and Elaine and Julie went flying through the air and tumbling over a small rise on the opposite side of the street. I couldn't believe it as I rushed off the bus. A large hand grabbed me by the collar, preventing me from running down the sidewalk to where they were hit by the car. Two teachers came running and yelling for everyone to get into their classrooms right away. We all did so but kept looking back into the direction of the accident.

The classroom was on the side of the school, which was equal to where the accident happened. We all were looking out the windows, as we watched the police, fire department, and ambulance arrive. With pits in our stomachs and all standing speechless, we just watched. The ambulance left, and in a short time, our teacher returned to the classroom. She had tears in her eyes as I observed her entering the room. She quietly asked everyone to take their seats.

"It is very difficult for me to explain the circumstances which have just taken place. Let's just sit for a moment."

In a minute or two, several other teachers came into our room. They stood in silence for a couple of minutes. Mrs. Shoemaker, our teacher, began with "Julie is in serious condition and is on her way to the hospital. Let's keep her in our thought and wish her the best." She again was silent and stared at her desk. Two of the other teachers stood by her with their hands on her shoulders. She then looked up at us and said, "I am so sorry, but Elaine died instantly on impact."

I couldn't breathe; my throat was stuck. I made no sound, but I could feel the tears rolling down my cheeks. I put my hand on the little desk beside me. I knew that Elaine would never again sit beside me with her tasteful answers, questions, and smiles. The teachers were loving and thoughtful as they made their way around the room. Parents were called, and most of the class went home. There were a couple of us left, and we would wait for the return trip home on the bus. It was a day in eternity, and all I could do was to touch the little desk and ask God why.

All I could think about were the words Elaine had given to me on January 17, just a couple of months prior. "Fred, if anything ever happens to me, take the Word of God to everyone you meet for as long as you live. Do this for me, please," she pleaded! At the time I thought it was a strange request as we knelt in the frozen corner of the schoolyard, with the blowing snow and no one around.

When I arrived home, I tried to talk to my parents about what had happened, but it was no good.

"Go do your chores and get firewood in," and so it was business as usual. It just seemed to take longer tonight. Supper couldn't be swallowed and sleep was elusive.

The next day at school was "I just don't care" day even if it was a Friday. The little desk beside me was moved to the back of the room. I went and got the desk and moved it back up beside mine. The teacher asked why I did that and I responded, "It seems like the right thing to do. I miss her and will miss her, probably forever. I promise to never forget her and all she means to me."

She just said she understood. Several class members came over by my desk, as if they were going to say something or that I perhaps had more to say. I could say nothing. They too seemed to want to stand by the little desk.

By the time we got home from school, it had started snowing. In the morning, it was still snowing. It just made chores and other work that much harder. After lunch I tried to talk to my mother about what had happened to Elaine, but she just said that she had no answers. Perhaps if I went out and cut wood, it would help to stay busy. Maybe that would help. It was snowing so hard you couldn't see the woods across the yard.

I went out, grabbed the saw, and went to the woodpile. I went to the stump where I had met messenger a year ago. Messenger, so I had called him since, had brought Pastor Peterson and Elaine a year ago into my life. "Why? Why?" I spoke quietly. "I have heard of the great things you do, God. I find it hard to ask of you because I am of such little importance. Let me trade my life for Elaine. I think that it would be a lot better for your people to have her around. I am going to walk into the face of this snowstorm, and whatever happens, it's on me. Let your hand do what is necessary. I have only known you for a year. I have nothing but myself. I give you me with the greatest hope that you would bring Elaine back." I whispered these words as I slowly cut a piece of wood. I will go to talk to God or, perhaps, Messenger. Maybe they're the same, but I didn't think so.

After I put the saw away, I went walking down the driveway. I was determined to walk day and night into the storm to talk to God and get the answers I needed! It was about a mile and a half to the end of the driveway. Trees packed the lane all the way. The snow was pounding down and the wind had drifted the lane with some two- and three-foot drifts. I walked slowly and looked at all the details as if I wouldn't see them again. The heavy snow tried to blur out the trees. I had walked about a third of the way down the lane, plowing through the drifts. I suddenly thought I saw something move on top of a power pole. "God, Messenger, Jesus," I whispered. I had never seen something like this before.

I continued to walk but now concentrating on the top of the power pole. "What form are you?" I asked. There was something and it was as big as me. It jumped off the pole; it was a bird, or was it? The wingspan was six or seven feet wide, and it was diving straight toward me. Surely it would fly away. I saw its face as it opened its beak. The next second it seemed to open itself up. I saw two huge claws extend forward and a furry, white, feathery mass of flapping wings as I hit

187

the snow facedown. I was struck with fear as I went as deep as I could go into the snow. I prepared for a claw or something to tear into my back as it had happened when I was four.

"Jesus, help me," I pleaded as I burrowed deeper into the snow. I dug toward the side of the lane where the snow was deeper. I stayed under the snow for a good long time. I hoped it couldn't see me. The fear, as my heart beat up into my throat.

"Jesus, I don't understand any of this," I confessed. "Protect me from this creature, but please help me understand. Please help me to find a way to…to go on I guess. There is no intent to challenge you but just to talk to you. I meant I was willing to trade my life for Elaine. Is this the way?"

I stayed under the snow. Nothing happened. I cried and I prayed. "How many times will you protect my life, God? Why, why, and for what purpose?" I waited for the creature to snatch me away. Nothing happened, but still I waited, waited for something. I came up out of the snow and looked around. The snow was still falling hard, but I saw no creature.

What had I seen? Why now and why this way? I had been determined to walk into the storm and talk to God.

Pastor Peterson had been picking me up and taking me to church for a year. I had at least an hour of time for a one-on-one. I could learn more in an hour with him than a month going to church. Had God sent this creature to stop me from my path, to cut me off? Had I displeased God? Was this Messenger in the form of a creature? It had distracted me as I found myself walking back to the farmstead. "So you don't need to talk to you Jesus in a special prayer? I can talk to you just regular? Do you always answer so dynamically? Elaine says you answer in all forms. She said if no one is talking to you and listening for you to answer, the world is a blur for them. She told me that she talks to you every day. I believe, I believe, that she is with you now. She said to be grateful, be respectful, and give you the glory in all things. I am going to do this and for Elaine and Pastor Peterson because you sent them to me, even for a short time."

Pastor Peterson often explained to me that you will come into contact with more people who will try to explain God away than people who will help you get closer to God. God really loves the little children and those who can have a childlike faith. You will find people, with more education, trying to give an explanation that man has done this or that. God helps mankind come up with all kinds of wonderful things, but is it too hard to give God some credit for helping someone invent something?

> And he made in Jerusalem engines, invented by cunning men, to be on the towers and upon the bulwarks, to shoot arrows and great stones withal. And his name spread far abroad; for he was marvelously helped, till he was strong. (2 Chronicles 26:15)

In a short time of conversation, I found myself back at the woodpile. "Father, protect me from that which I see and what I do not see," I whispered. I reflected back to all the dynamic things that I had been through and didn't even know God. A six-foot poison snake in my playpen, scarlet fever, a bottle of aspirin fed to me by my brother, whooping cough twice, exotic rooster attack, stranded in a snowstorm, nearly caught in a forest fire, and diphtheria. All the daily things we never recognize. I need God every day. *Take those times, all the people in the world*, I thought.

I never talked to my parents about that day, about God. They thought God was for some, but they believed in their own way. That I didn't understand, but I respected them for who they were. However, I did talk to Pastor Peterson about the ordeal. He told me that God would speak to his children in a thousand different ways. He may use a burning bush to animals, to other people, whom you have never known, or to rocks if he had to. He said if I had just walked away into the snowstorm, it would have been like throwing my life away.

"Try not to be so challenging toward God, or at least don't be foolish. Humble yourself before God when seeking answers. Boldly go forth when God instructs you to do so. The creature, the large snowy owl or whatever it was, kept you from continuing your path to who knows where. A predatory bird of that size would and could take on something even as big as itself, perhaps even you. Let the Holy Spirit guide you."

The Holy Spirit is God—just as God the Father is God and just as Jesus is God. Our Christian belief about the Trinity is that God is three Persons: the Father, the Son, and Holy Spirit. The Holy Spirit is the third Person of the Trinity. The Holy Spirit helps us in many ways, such as being our Teacher, helping us know when we are doing wrong, guiding us, helping us to know the truth, and giving us the power to live the Christian life and to tell others about Jesus.

God is calling his people to face evil in this world with the truth of Scripture and with boldness. When God made a covenant with Israel on Mount Sinai, he told them to have no false gods. In the days of Elijah, the children of Israel went after the false gods. Their sin led to the prophet Elijah challenging the false prophets (read 1 Kings 18:15).

The same thing happens in our lives, families, churches, and communities. When we make a commitment to live for God, we will face conflict with evil. Just like Elijah, God will give each of us power and wisdom through the Holy Spirit to confront whatever evil may stand in opposition to the plan of God.

Love in Christ, Fred

About the Author

❧

When Fred Blom was eleven years old, he was in a coma for six days after his appendix ruptured and poisoned his system. As he looked down at himself lying in a bed, he heard a voice call to him to come forth. He went to the voice and ended up in a beautiful place but totally not fitting in his mind.

During his time there, he was given an opportunity to ask anything he wanted. After much thought and looking around, he thought he had something he could ask for. He went over to a great tree and hopped up on a low branch.

"Great One, may I request something?" Fred asked.

"As it was offered!" Messenger replied.

"When I leave this place, give me something I can share someday with others, and keep this for my knowledge."

Suddenly there appeared a great vessel in front of him. It was as large as a person and as clear as polished glass.

"This represents a soul," Messenger instructed. "When you accept the King of Light, Jesus Christ, as your Savior, it becomes brilliant."

Suddenly a great brilliance filled the vessel. He heard music! He hopped off the branch and tried to look closer. It was incredible! Mankind chooses sin! A small swirl of vapor appeared above the vessel. It was dark! It went into the vessel and gradually turned the vessel black as ink.

"Mankind liked sin and continued to darken their soul even unto death," Messenger instructed. "Mankind looks upon all of the wrong things and misses what is important. Mankind looks at each other in sin, and sin judges—rich or poor, big or small, knowledge-able or not, red or yellow, black or white."

Suddenly, with a great burst, the vessel was brilliant again. "Then there would be those that call out for salvation from sin!" Messenger boomed! The King of Light, who sits on the right hand of the Ancient One has all things in his hands forever! Be of this light and live! Your soul will be of brilliance! Look beyond what your body sees!"